The Kids Book of
CANADA
AT WAR

WRITTEN BY

Elizabeth MacLeod

ILLUSTRATED BY

John Mantha

KIDS CAN PRESS

Dedication

With much admiration and gratitude to all the Canadians who have represented their country in conflicts within Canada and around the world, especially my father, Flight Lieutenant Duncan Rae MacLeod; my uncles Second Lieutenant Blair Anderson, Flight Lieutenant John MacLeod and Flying Officer James "Bud" Martin; my aunt Corporal Dorothy (Veinot) MacLeod; my cousin Corporal Kay Cattanach (Black); and Flight Lieutenant Howard Vandewater.

Acknowledgements

Many thanks to the staff at the Canadian War Museum who assisted with this book, including Dr. Tim Cook, First World War historian, Genevieve de Mahy, Jane Naisbitt and especially Dr. Dean F. Oliver, Director, Research and Exhibitions. I'm also grateful for the assistance of Alix McEwen, Reference Archivist, Library and Archives Canada; Ann ten Cate, Archivist, British Columbia Archives; Christine McClymont; Jocelyn Stoate; and Karen Virag.

Special thanks to everyone who provided artifacts and photos for the book, including Sandra Black, Janet Cattanach, Carol Cluff, Scott Dickinson, Cathi Duboisson, Rae MacLeod, Bryan Maloney and Samantha Swenson. Very special thanks also to the Scott family of Victoria, British Columbia, for allowing access to their family papers from World War I.

Time and again I realize how very, very lucky I am to work with editor Valerie Wyatt. She improved this book in so many ways and I'm extremely grateful for her skill, time, persistence and friendship. Thank you so much, Val. Special thanks also to Larry MacDonald for reviewing the manuscript so carefully and making such helpful suggestions. I also really appreciate the work of copy editor Kathy Vanderlinden and production editor Samantha Swenson.

Julia Naimska created a wonderful design for the book, John Mantha provided great illustrations and Karen Becker and Patricia Buckley obtained terrific photographs. Many thanks to you all.

I always appreciate the support of my Dad and brothers John and Douglas.
Thanks and love to Paul for his assistance as I battled with this manuscript.

Text © 2007 Elizabeth MacLeod
Illustrations © 2007 John Mantha

Kids Can Press acknowledges the financial support of the Government of Ontario, through the Ontario Media Development Corporation's Ontario Book Initiative; the Ontario Arts Council; the Canada Council for the Arts; and the Government of Canada, through the BPIDP, for our publishing activity.

Published in Canada by	Published in the U.S. by
Kids Can Press Ltd.	Kids Can Press Ltd.
29 Birch Avenue	2250 Military Road
Toronto, ON M4V 1E2	Tonawanda, NY 14150

www.kidscanpress.com

Edited by Valerie Wyatt
Designed by Julia Naimska
Printed and bound in Singapore

This book is smyth sewn casebound.

CM 07 0 9 8 7 6 5 4 3 2 1

Library and Archives Canada Cataloguing in Publication

MacLeod, Elizabeth
The kids book of Canada at war / Elizabeth MacLeod ;
John Mantha, illustrator.

Includes index.
ISBN 978-1-55453-003-8 (bound)

1. Canada—History, Military—Juvenile literature.
I. Mantha, John II. Title.

FC226.M35 2007   j355.00971   C2006-906850-X

Kids Can Press is a /orus™ Entertainment company

CONTENTS

CANADA AT WAR

Today Canada is known around the world for helping keep the peace in war-torn countries. But Canada's past is full of wars and battles, some as short as 15 minutes, such as the Battle of the Plains of Abraham, and others lasting many years, including World War II.

Not all the wars and battles described in this book took place in Canada. In fact, the last battle on Canadian soil was fought in 1885 — it was part of the Métis Rebellions. Since then, Canadian men and women have served in battles in many other countries, including the Korean War and the Gulf War.

Canadians go to war for many reasons: to protect their homes and culture, to help other nations and to stand up for human rights. Going to war can have many results. For instance, World War I and World War II changed Canada's place in the world. Our country had been a member of the British Commonwealth, with Great Britain making international decisions for it. After World War II, it became an independent country that spoke for itself.

Billy Bishop

War is a time of terrible tragedy and great loss. But it is also a time of incredible courage and determination. Laura Secord, who helped save Canada during the War of 1812, and Billy Bishop, the World War I flying ace, are well-known heroes who bravely served Canada.

Many other, lesser-known people also played important roles in Canada's wartime history. For instance, Georgina Pope (right) was a nurse during the South African (Boer) War and was the first Canadian to earn the Royal Red Cross medal. William Stephenson's work as one of World War II's most important spies was kept secret for many years to conceal his identity and protect him.

Throughout the book are suggestions for places you can visit to find out more about Canada's military history. From Fort Rodd Hill in Victoria, British Columbia, to the North Atlantic Aviation Museum in Gander, Newfoundland, you can learn a lot about Canadian wartime contributions. Canada's capital, Ottawa, is full of memorials and museums, including the Canadian War Museum. If you don't live near any of these places, check out their Web sites.

When war is necessary, Canadians have fearlessly fought for what they believe is right. But Canadians really excel at peacekeeping. After helping to set up the United Nations, Canada has worked for peace in such countries as Kosovo, Somalia and Haiti, as well as now providing disaster relief around the world.

Blayney Scott (second from left) of Victoria, British Columbia, fought in World War I. Find out more about him on pages 43 and 45.

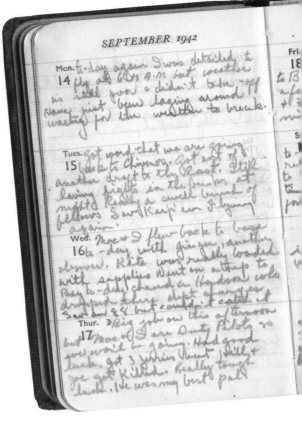

Fighter pilot Howard S. Vandewater of Toronto kept a diary during World War II. He was pleased on September 17, 1942, to hear three "Jerries" (Germans) had been shot down but devastated to lose his best friend.

More than 116 000 Canadians have died in military service. That's a large number considering Canada's population. We remember these brave Canadians each year on Remembrance Day, November 11. It is important to honour all those who have served in the air, on land and on the sea to protect Canada or keep peace around the world.

WE STAND ON GUARD

At the Canadian War Museum in Ottawa, you can see weapons, uniforms and medals from many of the wars in which Canadians have taken part. A life-size model of a World War I trench puts you in the midst of the conflict, while a mock-up of the D-Day landing in World War II lets you see exactly how the brave Canadians advanced.

The best day to visit the museum? Definitely November 11. A window has been carefully positioned so that at 11 a.m. on Remembrance Day each year, the sun shines through onto the gravestone of Canada's Unknown Soldier. This soldier represents all Canadians with no known grave who died in any of Canada's wars.

FIRST CONTACT

Long before the first European explorers ever set foot in Canada, there were battles going on here. Most First Nations groups had some type of military force and fought from time to time to defend their trade routes, homes and territories.

The coming of the Europeans gave First Nations people even more reason to fight — it soon became clear that the newcomers wanted the land for themselves. The fighting between the two groups would continue on and off for almost 900 years.

The Vikings Arrive

Vikings (Norsemen) first landed in what is now Newfoundland around the year 1000. They were met by the Beothuk, an Aboriginal people living there.

At first, relations were friendly, but then skirmishes broke out. After many deaths due to trade disagreements, the Vikings abandoned their settlements (one is now known as L'Anse aux Meadows) and sailed home.

More Europeans

About 500 years passed before Europeans returned to Canada. In 1534, explorer Jacques Cartier sailed toward the mouth of the St. Lawrence River. There he encountered a group of Iroquois and their chief Donnacona.

Champlain and the Fur Trade

The French explorer Samuel de Champlain came next. In 1608, he set up a trading post on the former site of Stadacona (which had since been abandoned) and called it Quebec. Soon he was trading with the Huron people and helping them fight their enemy, the Iroquois.

In 1609, Champlain and some of his men joined the Hurons in an attack on the Iroquois. The French had muskets (early rifles). It was the first time guns had been used against the Iroquois, and three of them were killed.

Early explorers used astrolabes like this one to help navigate.

As the Iroquois watched, Cartier erected a huge wooden cross and claimed the land for France. Donnacona didn't understand what Cartier was saying, but he could see what Cartier was doing, and he was very angry. Donnacona was also unhappy when Cartier insisted on taking the chief's two sons back to France with him.

back: all but one had died. That turned the Iroquois against the French, and fighting broke out. Cartier and his men departed — the French would not return for another 50 years.

Cartier Returns

In 1535, Cartier sailed to Canada again, this time landing at the Iroquois village of Stadacona. Donnacona was pleased to have his sons back, but he continued to mistrust the Frenchman, especially when Cartier insisted on travelling farther up the St. Lawrence against the chief's wishes.

After overwintering in the Iroquois village of Hochelaga (where Montreal is today), Cartier returned to France in the spring of 1536. He took with him ten Iroquois, including Donnacona. When Cartier returned to Canada on a third trip, in 1541, he brought none of them

This drawing by Champlain shows him with the Hurons fighting the Iroquois.

New France Expands

France's territory in Canada was known as New France, and French fur traders wanted to make it larger. In 1642, a settlement, Ville-Marie, was started on an island in the St. Lawrence River now known as Montreal. The island was controlled by Iroquois, who launched attack after attack to drive the settlers away. The settlers fought back and held onto their island settlement.

Canadian Courage

Nicknamed "the Angel of the Colony," nurse Jeanne Mance was vital to the survival of Ville-Marie (now Montreal). She arrived there in 1642 and founded a hospital to treat people injured in battles with the Iroquois. You can visit a museum in Montreal dedicated to her.

Sainte-Marie was rebuilt and you can visit it today.

Sainte-Marie Among the Hurons

The French continued to befriend the Huron people and fight with the Iroquois. French missionaries built a settlement called Sainte-Marie Among the Hurons, near today's Midland, Ontario. From 1639 to 1649, the village was a base for missionaries in the area.

When the Iroquois began attacking nearby Huron villages, the missionaries burned Sainte-Marie to keep the religious items it held from falling into Iroquois hands.

Long Sault

New France made a truce with the Iroquois, but it didn't last long. By the late 1650s, the two sides were fighting again.

In 1660, Adam Dollard des Ormeaux led 60 French and Aboriginal men up the Ottawa River. They intended to fight any Iroquois hunters they found. At Long Sault Rapids, Dollard and his men ran into a huge force of Iroquois who were on their way to attack Montreal. Dollard's group hung on for about seven days, but all were killed. So many Iroquois were killed or wounded that the attack on Montreal was called off.

In 1665, 1100 trained soldiers arrived from France. Although the soldiers never fought a major battle with the Iroquois and left after only three years, their presence was enough to stop the fighting. In 1667, the Iroquois signed another peace treaty with the French.

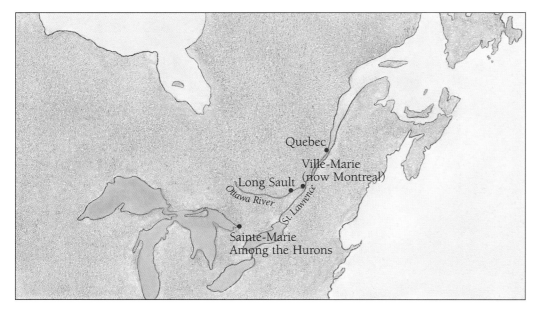

Europeans vs. First Nations

"They come like foxes through the woods. They attack like lions. They take flight like birds, disappearing before they have really appeared." That's how Jérôme Lalemant, a French missionary, described Iroquois warriors. Europeans had never seen battle tactics like those the First Nations people used.

Soldiers from Europe were used to fighting in long lines on large, open battlefields. They attacked only when their leader gave a signal. First Nations people fought by luring their enemies into the woods and ambushing them. They also made surprise attacks and raids.

The European soldiers came equipped with muskets and bayonets (daggers attached to the muskets). They also had cannons, although these were used sparingly because ammunition was limited.

First Nations people did not have guns. They used the tomahawk (an axe-like weapon with a deadly blade) and clubs, some with spikes on them. Their main weapons were bows and arrows. Arrows flew silently through the air, and so were excellent for surprise attacks. They could also be launched much more quickly than slow-to-load muskets. As well, arrows could be lit with fire to ignite whatever they hit.

Germ Warfare

The First Nations people battled not only the Europeans but also the diseases they brought with them. Smallpox, measles, chicken pox and other European diseases swept through First Nations settlements, killing thousands.

Most First Nations warriors were incredibly accurate shots. But there was one big difference between guns and arrows — arrow wounds were rarely fatal, while gun wounds almost always were.

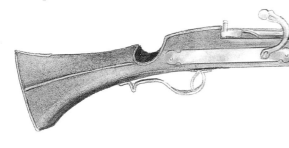

European muskets were a deadly weapon against First Nations people.

Forts

One of the best ways to protect yourself from enemies is to build a wall. By the 1400s, the Huron and Iroquois people were constructing high walls around their settlements.

Tall tree trunks woven together with saplings made strong fortress walls surrounding their villages. Sometimes lookouts were posted around the top of the wall to keep a sharp watch for possible attackers.

Europeans also built forts in Canada, but they were more like the castles they knew back home. Most were on rivers or lakes, since food, ammunition and other supplies had to be brought by canoe or ship.

FUR TRADE BATTLES

France and England had been enemies for many years. In the 1600s, they had something new to fight over: beaver pelts from Canada. Hats made of felted beaver fur were the latest fashion in Europe. Everyone wanted one.

At first, the French were the only fur traders in Canada. But it wasn't long before they had competition from their enemy, the English.

The French traded knives, pots and other goods for furs.

Trading Post Wars

In 1670, the English set up trading posts in northern Canada, on the shores of Hudson Bay and James Bay. Some Aboriginal people began taking their furs to the English posts instead of trading with the French.

The French were not about to let the English butt in on such a rich opportunity without a fight. French soldiers attacked the English forts and captured some of them. Over the next 40 years, these northern fur-trading posts changed hands back and forth between the French and English — usually after lots of fighting.

Battling the Settlers

Early in 1690, the governor of New France, Louis de Buade, Comte de Frontenac, sent a force of French settlers and First Nations soldiers south to attack the English settlements in New York and New England. He wanted to stop the American colonies from providing weapons to the Iroquois in their battles with New France. Many English settlers were

> "I HAVE NO REPLY TO MAKE TO YOUR GENERAL, OTHER THAN FROM THE MOUTHS OF MY CANNON AND MUSKETS."
>
> *Governor Frontenac to English invaders*

killed in the raids, but this only made the English more determined to fight back.

Later in 1690, an English fleet sailed up from Boston and demanded Quebec's surrender. Frontenac refused. Luckily for the colony, winter set in early and the English were forced to retreat.

Back on the Bay

Fighting also continued between the French and English on Hudson Bay as they battled for control of the fur trade. In one famous battle in 1697, Pierre Le Moyne d'Iberville, found his ship separated from the rest of the French ships. He took on three English ships alone and, against all odds, won the battle.

French vs. Iroquois

The peace treaty between the French and Iroquois (page 8) lasted from 1667 until 1680. Then vicious fighting broke out again. Innocent people were killed on both sides. The French invaded the territory of the Seneca people in 1687 and burned all their villages. The Seneca's allies, the Iroquois, retaliated two years later. Fifteen hundred warriors attacked French settlers in Lachine, just west of Montreal. They killed 24 and later tortured more than 60.

But by 1700, the Iroquois were too weakened to continue battling the French. Constant fighting as well as diseases they'd caught from the Europeans had killed many. The Iroquois could no longer control their vast territory. In 1701, they signed a peace treaty with New France and most of its First Nations allies. In exchange, New France agreed to allow the Iroquois to continue to trade in the interior of Canada. The fighting between the French and Iroquois was over.

Canadian Courage

When the Iroquois attacked Fort de Verchères, on October 22, 1692, Madeleine Jarret's parents were away on business. With the help of one old soldier, the 14-year-old girl took command. Madeleine yelled and waved her arms to make the raiders think there were many soldiers inside. Then she signalled for help from nearby forts.

All night Madeleine stayed awake, scanning the fort's walls for attackers. The Iroquois gave up the next day. Madeleine de Verchères, as she came to be known, saved the fort and became a heroine of New France.

Much of the fighting in early Canada was over control of the fur trade. Beaver pelts like the one you see here were in great demand in Europe.

EAST COAST BATTLES

Quebec and Montreal were just two of France's settlements in Canada. France also controlled much of the east coast, which we now call the Maritime provinces.

When France and England were at war in Europe, their battles spilled over into Canada — including the east coast settlements of the French. They were an easy target for the English colonies to the south.

New Technology

The French territory on the east coast was called Acadia. It consisted of parts of present-day Nova Scotia, New Brunswick and Prince Edward Island. Acadia also included settlements in Newfoundland, where the English had colonies as well. The French were at Placentia (below), on the west side of the Avalon Peninsula, while the English were in St. John's, on the east side.

The English feared the French would attack St. John's by ship. But in late 1696, French troops surprised them by attacking overland. They seemed to have done the impossible, travelling across the Avalon Peninsula through heavy snow. It turns out the French had a secret weapon: snowshoes. The French took almost every English settlement in their path, including St. John's.

What Happened When? Acadia was attacked many times in the colony's 150-year history.

1613	1628	1632	1654	1670	1690
English soldiers from Virginia to the south attack Acadia.	*The English capture Acadia (and Quebec).*	*England returns Acadia (and Quebec) to France.*	*England captures Port-Royal and again controls Acadia.*	*France regains control of Acadia.*	*English soldiers attack Acadia again — as revenge for a raid from Quebec.*

Easy Target Again

Acadia was attacked again and again by the English between 1702 and 1713, as part of Queen Anne's War, being fought in Europe. When the English captured the French settlement of Port-Royal in 1710, they renamed it Fort Anne and called the area Annapolis Royal.

Queen Anne's War ended in 1713. France paid for its losses in Europe by giving up its claim to Hudson Bay, as well as most of Acadia. These territories passed into English control.

The French were left with New France, Île Royale (now Cape Breton Island), Île St. Jean (Prince Edward Island) and the coast of New Brunswick. But the British were now in control of most of Acadia.

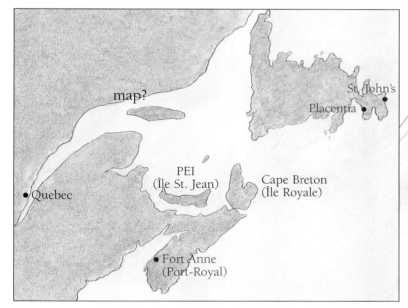

British (red) and French (black) territory in 1713.

Canadian Courage

Marie de la Tour is one of Acadia's most famous women. When the king of France put her husband and Charles de Menou d'Aulnay in charge of Acadia, the two men could not get along and became bitter enemies.

In April 1645, d'Aulnay learned that de la Tour's husband was away and attacked their fort. Marie de la Tour commanded her 45 soldiers bravely, but d'Aulnay overpowered them. Only when he finally promised to spare the lives of her troops did de la Tour agree to surrender.

But d'Aulnay had lied — he hanged de la Tour's soldiers, much to her grief. She died in prison, but her courage earned her the nickname "Lioness of Acadia."

1696/1697

The French capture the English settlements around St. John's, Newfoundland.

1704

Acadia is attacked by soldiers from New England. The raiders attack again the next year and in 1707.

1710

Acadia is attacked by 3500 British soldiers. (England became Great Britain in 1707.) The 300 Acadian defenders are overpowered.

1713

As part of a treaty ending a European war, France gives up much of Acadia to Britain. Britain changes the name of the area from Port-Royal to Annapolis Royal. Thirty years of peace for Acadia follow.

1744

The French attack Annapolis Royal, but the raid finally fails when supply ships don't arrive in time.

continued on next page

The Acadian "Threat"

In 1713, French Acadia came under British control, but the Acadians still thought of themselves as French, not British. They avoided or ignored the British. For instance, when taxes were due, the Acadians found lots of excuses for not paying them. And when the British urged the Acadians to promise to fight for Britain if war should break out, the Acadians refused. They didn't want to have to fight French soldiers.

In the 1740s, Britain and France were at war again. The British began to worry that the Acadians would help the French. They again attempted to force the Acadians to swear to fight for Britain.

Battles on Water

When French and British ships clashed at sea, their main weapon was the cannon. Because it was almost impossible to take accurate aim with these big guns, ships had to be close together to do any damage. Cannonballs that did hit a ship could punch holes in its side, break the mast or spray the deck with splinters.

When two ships neared each other, each would try to be first to fire a "broadside." That was a blast from all the cannons on one side of the ship at exactly the same time. A battle could often be won by a single broadside.

What Happened When?

1745
The French Fortress of Louisbourg (page 16) is captured by the British.

1748
Louisbourg is returned to the French as part of a war treaty.

1755–1762
Expulsion of the Acadians.

1758
The British capture Louisbourg again.

1763
The Treaty of Paris ends the Seven Years' War. France gives up almost all of its land in North America, including Acadia.

1764
The Acadians are allowed to return.

The Expulsion of the Acadians

British leaders in Acadia didn't trust the Acadians not to help France in battles against Britain. So on September 5, 1755, the British ordered the French men in the area to gather at the town of Grand Pré. With rifles pointed at them, the men were told that they and their families must leave Acadia, that their land and livestock now belonged to the British and that their homes would be destroyed.

"When the men and boys in the Church were read the Order, they were speechless with terror," one Acadian recounted. "Some tried to force the door, but they were overawed by the muskets of their guards."

Some Acadians were killed as soldiers forced them onto ships. Husbands and wives were separated from each other and from their children. Many never saw one another again. As they sailed away, sobbing and wailing, they could see their homes going up in flames.

The British ships took the Acadians to the American colonies, to France, England and the Caribbean. Many died of disease on the tightly packed ships. A few Acadians managed to hide in the woods to escape being taken onto the ships. But even when the danger passed, they could not go back to their ruined farms and had to find new homes.

The expulsions lasted until 1762. By then, 10 000 Acadians had been deported. Almost none remained. Acadia no longer existed.

In 1764, the ban on Acadians was lifted. About 3000 Acadians returned to Nova Scotia. But their land had been given away. They had to begin new lives in New Brunswick.

In 2003, the Canadian government issued a proclamation recognizing what the Acadians had endured and acknowledging that it was wrong.

The expulsion, or deportation, of the Acadians shattered the lives of thousands. But they worked hard to preserve their culture and memories. Today more than 30 percent of the population of New Brunswick is Acadian.

WE STAND ON GUARD

Near Wolfville, Nova Scotia, Grand Pré National Historic Park commemorates the Acadians and their expulsion. At Annapolis Royal, you can find out more about Acadia at the military museum in Fort Anne Historic National Park.

LOUISBOURG

The town of Louisbourg on Cape Breton Island, Nova Scotia, became France's main military base and port on the Atlantic coast. At its busiest in the 1750s, it held a population of about 4000. It was one of the largest towns of New France and one of the busiest harbours in North America.

The French thought Louisbourg could protect the entrance to the St. Lawrence River and Quebec. In 1719, they began building walls around the town to make it stronger. By the 1740s, it was a fortress surrounded by tall ramparts topped with cannons.

The work cost a fortune, and the French king, Louis XV, for whom the town was named, complained bitterly about the price. Even with the new walls, Louisbourg was still at risk of attack. It wasn't high enough above the surrounding area, and the nearby hills were too close.

The fortress of Louisbourg was finally finished in 1745 — just before it was attacked. The British set up their cannons on the hills and stopped anyone and anything from going in or out of the fortress. After six weeks, with little food or ammunition left, Louisbourg had to surrender. The people inside were deported to France.

France got Louisbourg back in 1748 as part of a war treaty. The townspeople returned and rebuilt their damaged fortress. In 1758, the British were back. They far outnumbered the French, but the French soldiers held them off for two months. Once again the British siege technique was successful.

The British spent five months blowing up the fortress so the French could never use it again. Abandoned in 1768, the town lay desolate until the 1900s, when people began to show interest in the historic ruins. Part of the fortress has been rebuilt as a reminder of Canadian life and military battles during the 1700s.

Cape Breton
(Île Royale)

Louisbourg

"ARE THE STREETS BEING PAVED WITH GOLD OVER THERE? I FULLY EXPECT TO AWAKE ONE MORNING IN MY PALACE AT VERSAILLES AND SEE THE WALLS OF THE LOUISBOURG FORTRESS RISING ABOVE THE HORIZON."

King Louis XV of France

DID YOU KNOW

In the 1700s, the flag France flew over its colonies, such as Louisbourg, was a white flag. When French soldiers won a battle, they also hoisted their white flag on the enemy's flagpole. As a result, a white flag became a worldwide symbol for surrender.

Inside the Barracks

Being a soldier at Louisbourg was tough. The men were badly paid and didn't have enough to eat. Some of the soldiers were under 16, and most were far away from their homes in France. They felt isolated, and they hated the climate with its freezing winters and thick fogs.

The rotting barracks where the men lived were full of rats. Each room slept 12 to 16 men, two to a bunk. As the governor of the town said, "The straw on which they sleep is changed only once a year, and this results in so many insects in their quarters that the majority prefer to sleep on the ramparts during the summer."

The officers received much better food, as well as better and bigger living quarters. No wonder the soldiers often rebelled.

WE STAND ON GUARD

Today you can tour the fortress in Louisbourg. You'll see massive stone walls and more than 60 reconstructed buildings. Amazingly, that's less than one-quarter of the original fortress! When you visit, be sure to talk to the adults and kids dressed in historical costumes and find out what life was like there 250 years ago.

In 1995, history fans re-enacted the 1745 siege of Louisbourg.

PLAINS OF ABRAHAM

In 1759, the future was looking very uncertain for New France. The French were outnumbered. The British forces had three times as many ships, four times as many trained soldiers and ten times as much money.

For weeks, British general James Wolfe and his soldiers had bombarded Quebec City. But the Marquis de Montcalm, leader of the French forces, fought them off from behind Quebec's high walls. The city had good natural defences, too — it sat above the St. Lawrence River, high atop steep cliffs.

British Risk Taker

By September, Wolfe knew his time was running out — winter was coming. He realized it would be risky to get his soldiers up the cliffs on which the city was perched. Risky or, according to Montcalm, impossible: "We do not need to imagine that the enemy has wings so that in one night they can cross the river, disembark, and climb the obstructed cliffs."

But Wolfe thought otherwise. On September 13, 1759, just after midnight, 4500 British troops slipped up the river to a small cove close to Quebec City. They scrambled up the cliff, grabbing at trees and roots. They even managed to haul up two small cannons.

Disaster at Dawn

As the sun rose that morning, the French were shocked to find British red coats lined up on the Plains of Abraham, a field just outside the city walls. Now it was Montcalm's move. He called in 5000 troops who were stationed an hour's march away. The soldiers had already been on duty all night. They were not only tired but hungry, since food was scarce in the war-torn area. Exhausted, they headed toward the Plains of Abraham.

Should Montcalm wait for additional back-up soldiers? Delaying might mean more British soldiers could arrive, too. "If we give them enough time to establish themselves," Montcalm told one of his commanders, "we will never be able to attack with the kind of army we have." Montcalm had to decide quickly — the British were already firing on his men.

Montcalm assembled his French Canadian soldiers (called Canadiens), First Nations allies and French troops. At 10 a.m., he gave the order to attack.

The Seven Years' War Begins

The Battle of the Plains of Abraham was just one of many conflicts in the Seven Years' War. How long was this war? Would you believe nine years? It lasted from 1756 to 1763 in Europe but actually started in North America in 1754. The war was waged between Britain and its allies and France and its allies and was the first "world war."

The Seven Years' War was also the final conflict between the British and the French for control of North America. The war started in the Ohio Valley in the United States but spilled out into Acadia (page 12), the Great Lakes, Louisbourg (page 16) and New France.

The Battle Begins

The French soldiers and Canadiens hadn't trained together. Some fired their muskets too soon, others advanced too quickly. The British soldiers on the plains outside the city were trained to obey orders and fight in formation. They stood motionless in their lines, waiting for the order to fire. When the French side was just 37 m (120 ft.) away, the order came. The British soldiers fired.

Many French soldiers fell, dead or wounded. Their lines broke up in confusion. The English pressed forward with bayonets. The French troops scattered, chased by Scottish soldiers waving heavy, double-edged broadswords. One of the Canadiens said later: "I can remember the Scotch Highlanders flying wildly after us, with streaming plaids, bonnets and large swords — like so many infuriated demons."

DID YOU KNOW

The Plains of Abraham may be named after Abraham Martin, a French sailor and farmer who at one time owned the land.

This Scottish broadsword was used at the Battle of the Plains of Abraham.

British soldiers advance in this modern-day battle re-enactment.

The British took over Quebec City after the defeat of the French forces.

The Battle Ends

The Battle of the Plains of Abraham was over in a mere 15 minutes. The British had won. Montcalm and Wolfe were both fatally wounded. In all, 1300 French and British soldiers lay dead or wounded. Would the French launch another attack? No. There was little food inside Quebec's walls, and the bombing earlier in the year had destroyed much of the city. Quebec surrendered on September 18.

End of an Era

The Battle of the Plains of Abraham marked a turning point in Canadian history. It was not the last battle fought on the Plains of Abraham — another French–British battle took place there in 1760, and this time the French won. And it was not the last battle fought over who was to control Canada.

But the British victory in 1759 still changed Canada. New France came under British control and became known as British North America. More English-speaking people began to arrive.

Canadian Courage

The leader of the French forces on the Plains of Abraham, Louis-Joseph de Montcalm, joined the army when he was just nine years old, in 1721. By the time he was 17, he was a captain. At age 44, he was made a major-general and sent to New France. There, Montcalm captured a number of British forts.

James Wolfe, general for the British troops, became a soldier in 1740 at age 13. In 1758, he took part in the assault on Louisbourg (page 16). He was put in charge of the large British force sent to Quebec City the next year. But by then he was sick, which may be why his officers found him indecisive and bad-tempered.

Montcalm and Wolfe were both wounded just as the battle of the Plains of Abraham started. Wolfe lived long enough to know that his side was winning. He was buried in Westminster Abbey in London, England — you can still see his monument there.

Montcalm died the night after the battle. When he was told he could not survive, he said, "Good — then I will not live to see the British enter Quebec." There were no more coffins left in Quebec City, so Montcalm was buried in a crater blasted in the earth during the attack.

Montcalm   Wolfe

No Peace for the British

Even with the French gone from North America, the British soon had new enemies to contend with.

First Nations people were unhappy with the British settlements on their territory. In 1763, they began attacking them. So the British issued the Royal Proclamation of 1763, which set out a large territory for First Nations people.

The proclamation angered people in America. They wanted to move into First Nations territory, but the proclamation blocked them. It also established the province of Quebec. When the British gave more rights and land to Quebec in 1774, the Americans decided to invade Canada.

On November 12, 1775, the Americans captured Montreal. Next they headed towards Quebec.

Despite a fierce snowstorm, on December 31, the Americans attacked the city. They stumbled about in the thick snow as the British fired on them. The Americans lost the battle badly, and about 100 of them were killed. The snow was so thick that bodies were still being found the next spring.

By July 2, 1776, all the Americans were gone from Canada. But they would be back.

WE STAND ON GUARD

At Battlefields Park in Quebec City, the story of the Battle of the Plains of Abraham is brought to life with monuments and plaques. You can see guns and uniforms from the battle, as well as explore the old prison.

The Americans (left) attacked Quebec City but lost the battle.

The Seven Years' War Ends

The last North American battle in the Seven Years' War was fought at Signal Hill, Newfoundland, in 1762. In 1763, the war formally ended with the Treaty of Paris. Britain kept Canada, while France gave up all of its territory in North America except the islands of St-Pierre and Miquelon, off Newfoundland, which it still owns. The Seven Years' War ended more than 150 years of fighting between Britain and France. This map shows Canada in 1763. The green area was controlled by the Hudson's Bay Company.

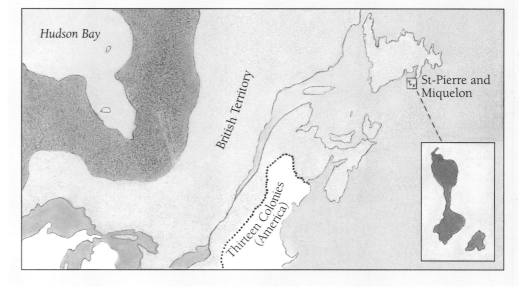

Hudson Bay

British Territory

St-Pierre and Miquelon

Thirteen Colonies (America)

WAR OF 1812

Surprisingly, the War of 1812 had nothing to do with Canada — at first. It started because the United States was angry with Great Britain. The British had been stopping and searching American ships, looking for British soldiers and cargo they considered illegal. Britain's colony of Canada was a closer and easier target, and the United States attacked.

The Americans had fought for their independence from Great Britain less than 40 years earlier. They thought that when they marched into Canada, people would welcome them, eager to break free from the British. But the Americans were in for a big surprise.

Outnumbered!

Most of the fighting during the War of 1812 took place along the American–Canadian border, in today's Ontario and Quebec. The Americans far outnumbered the Canadians. But Canadians were fighting for their lives and homes. They were much more determined than the Americans, who came from faraway states such as Kentucky. As well, thanks to British general Isaac Brock, the Canadians were well prepared.

Battle Fake-out

When the British attacked Fort Detroit in August 1812, they had less than half the soldiers of the American defenders. So General Brock planned the attack carefully.

Brock knew the Americans were terrified of the First Nations fighters. So he and First Nations leader Tecumseh put the First Nations men up front, where the Americans couldn't miss seeing them. Tecumseh also had his men march by several times so it would look as if there were more of them. The Americans surrendered Detroit without a fight.

Canadian Courage

Sir Isaac Brock had seen the War of 1812 coming ten years earlier. He improved Canada's defences so that his soldiers would be ready. Although often outnumbered, General Brock's soldiers were inspired by his courage. He became known as "the man who saved Canada."

"A more ... gallant Warrior does not I believe exist," is how Brock described First Nations leader Tecumseh. First Nations people fought on Britain's side in the War of 1812 because Tecumseh thought the British would help him defend his people's land. This Shawnee chief fought bravely in many important battles.

First Nations soldiers used tomahawks (above) and bows and arrows.

Secord and de Salaberry

Many people in Canada showed their bravery and love for their country in the War of 1812. Laura Secord was one of them. In June 1813, American officers took over the home of Laura Secord, who lived in Queenston, Ontario. They demanded to be fed and put up overnight. When the officers thought she couldn't hear their conversation, they boasted about making a surprise attack.

But Secord was listening. The next day, she struggled through forests and swamps to warn the British. Thanks to her courage, 116 British, Canadian and First Nation soldiers ambushed the 500 Americans three days later and won the Battle of Beaver Dams.

Lieutenant-Colonel Charles-Michel d'Irumberry de Salaberry led a regiment to victory at the Battle of Châteauguay in October 1813. His men were greatly outnumbered, but he positioned them carefully and fooled the Americans into thinking there were many more. The Americans retreated. De Salaberry had saved Montreal from attack.

LAURA SECORD LEGENDARY PATRIOT
HÉROÏNE LÉGENDAIRE

CANADA 42

What Happened When?

For almost two years, the Canadian and American armies won and lost battles and gained and gave up territory in the War of 1812. Here are some of the most important events.

June 18, 1812	October 13, 1812	April 27, 1813	May 27, 1813	June 5, 1813	June 24, 1813
The United States declares war on Britain and prepares to invade Canada, Britain's colony. Two months later, General Isaac Brock captures Fort Detroit.	*At the Battle of Queenston Heights, the Americans almost defeat the British, but 80 Mohawk hold them off. General Brock is killed.*	*Americans attack York (now Toronto). When the British realize they can no longer defend the fort, they explode their ammunition supplies, killing about 250 Americans.*	*The British and Canadians resist fiercely but lose Fort George, at Niagara-on-the-Lake, Ontario.*	*British and Canadian soldiers win the Battle of Stoney Creek. This ends the American attempt to conquer that part of Ontario.*	*Thanks to Laura Secord's warning and courageous First Nations warriors, the British and Canadians defeat the Americans at Beaver Dams.*

continued on next page

Soldiers vs. Civilians

A soldier's life in the War of 1812 was hard. Food was often scarce because the heavy supply carts couldn't get through the rough, narrow roads. Clothes were in short supply and so was shelter. Soldiers couldn't get enough rest between battles, so many became sick. More men died of disease than battle wounds — that was true of most wars until the late 1800s.

Local people were unfriendly to the soldiers, too, even to the British soldiers who were protecting them. No wonder — when soldiers were hungry or cold, they stole what they wanted. Livestock and crops were taken for food, and fence rails burned for warmth. As well, homes were destroyed as the two sides advanced and retreated.

Who Won?

The War of 1812 finally ended in December 1814. America and Canada would never fight each other again. Britain and the United States signed a treaty returning all territory that had been taken. Neither side won, but the First Nations people lost heavily. They had fought bravely for the British, but Britain did nothing to protect the First Nations' land.

Although the War of 1812 decided little, it was still an important Canadian event. Canada had beaten back an American invasion. That outcome would encourage Canada to dream of becoming an independent country.

Major battles in the War of 1812

LOWER CANADA
Ottawa River
Georgian Bay
Lake Huron
UPPER CANADA
Montreal
Châteauguay
Crysler's Farm
St. Lawrence River
Plattsburgh
Lake Champlain
Fort York
Lake Ontario
Fort Detroit
Moraviantown
Stoney Creek
Beaver Dams
Fort George
Fort Niagara
Queenston Heights
Lundy's Lane
U.S.A.
Lake Erie
Put-in-Bay

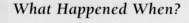

This sword was used during the War of 1812.

What Happened When?

September 10, 1813
American ships defeat the British in the Battle of Put-in-Bay, on Lake Erie.

October 5, 1813
At the Battle of Moraviantown, the British retreat, leaving First Nations leader Tecumseh and his warriors to face the Americans alone. Tecumseh is killed.

October 26, 1813
Lieutenant-Colonel Charles-Michel d'Irumberry de Salaberry beats the Americans at the Battle of Châteauguay, near Montreal.

November 11, 1813
The British and Canadians are outnumbered almost three to one at the Battle of Crysler's Farm. But they force the Americans to retreat. This defeat and the one at Châteauguay persuade the Americans to give up their plan to attack Montreal.

December 16, 1813
The Americans are forced to abandon Fort George. The British also capture Fort Niagara, across the river.

The Coloured Corps

A former slave in the United States, Richard Pierpoint had come to Canada in the late 1700s and had become a wealthy farmer. When the War of 1812 broke out, he felt it was time to fight for his new homeland.

Black people weren't allowed to fight in the same regiments as white soldiers, so Pierpoint asked the British to create a unit of "coloured" (Black) soldiers. He was one of 30 soldiers in the Coloured Corps, which fought bravely at Queenston Heights and Fort George.

Military College

After the War of 1812, Canada felt a need to improve military training. The Royal Military College was founded in 1874 in Kingston, Ontario, to train officers. The school is still in operation today.

WE STAND ON GUARD

Southern Ontario has many War of 1812 sites you can visit. If you want a good view of the Niagara Falls area, where many battles took place, climb the 235 steps to the top of Brock's Monument. You can visit Laura Secord Homestead, near Niagara Falls, where her famous walk began. Fort George in Niagara-on-the-Lake is set up as if the War of 1812 is about to break out. The Battle of Stoney Creek is re-enacted on that site each year.

There are more original War of 1812 buildings at Fort York in Toronto than anywhere else in Canada. A memorial and cannons mark a battle that took place at Crysler's Farm, along the St. Lawrence River, west of Cornwall. You can find out more about the battle at nearby Upper Canada Village. Fort Henry, also open to visitors, was built at Kingston to guard access to the Great Lakes.

July 25, 1814
One of the bloodiest battles of the War of 1812 is fought at Lundy's Lane, near Niagara Falls. About 640 British and Canadians and 740 Americans are killed or wounded before the Americans retreat.

August 24, 1814
British troops invade Washington, D.C. They burn down the White House and several other buildings.

September 11, 1814
The British strike into upper New York state but are defeated at Plattsburgh on Lake Champlain.

December 24, 1814
The Treaty of Ghent is signed by Britain and the United States, ending the War of 1812. (The treaty was named after the town in Belgium where it was signed.)

MUSKETS AND CANNONS

The War of 1812 was fought on land and on the water. Land battles involved ambushes, skirmishes in open fields or woods, as well as assaults on forts. Ships fought each other or attacked forts. Different types of battle required different weapons.

Not-So-Trusty Musket

The gun used during the War of 1812 was the musket, a long-barrelled gun that a shooter steadied on his shoulder. Loading a musket took many steps.

First, the soldier pulled back the flint, a small piece of quartz that could be made to spark.

The soldier then poured some gunpowder into a little pan on the outside of the gun barrel and closed a steel plate over the pan.

The soldier poured more gunpowder into the musket's barrel. Then he added a lead ball and rammed everything down the barrel.

To fire the gun, the soldier first pulled back the flint, then lifted the musket to his shoulder and pulled the trigger. That made the flint hit the steel over the pan full of gunpowder, causing a spark to fall into the pan. There'd be a blinding flash as the powder caught fire. It ignited the powder in the gun barrel, sending the lead ball flying.

This whole process took a well-trained soldier about 20 seconds. Muskets were heavy, so soldiers had to be very strong to repeatedly aim and fire them. As well, the gun had a dangerous kickback when fired that could injure the shooter. And even in the hands of a crack shot, the musket had a firing distance of less than half the length of a football field. Beyond that, targets were out of range.

This costumed soldier at Fort George demonstrates how muskets were fired. Note the cannonballs on the left.

Big Guns

The American and British sides used a number of cannons, but the most popular were "6 pounders," "9 pounders" and "12 pounders." The names described the weight of the cannonballs the cannons fired, about 2.7 kg, 4 kg and 5.5 kg.

Soldiers practised firing cannons so they could do it quickly in battle. One gunner cleaned the cannon barrel, then another wiped it with a wet sponge — they didn't want a spark to cause an explosion when they weren't ready. Gunpowder was loaded in, then the cannonball, or "shot" (see box this page). Finally, the wick was added and lit.

Cannons in forts were large, heavy weapons that fired straight ahead and shot non-exploding ammunition. Stationary "mortars" and movable "howitzers" fired in an arc over fort walls to reach inside fortresses. They used exploding ammunition and weren't as big as cannons.

Shoot the Shot

Cannons could be loaded with different kinds of ammunition depending on the battle. Sometimes they were packed with heated cannonballs. When this "hot shot" hit ships, fort walls or other structures, it often started a fire. Two cannonballs linked with heavy chain were known as chain shot and could rip a ship's sail or break its mast.

Soldiers could also use musket balls — smaller balls packed into a container the size of a large juice can. When the container was fired, the musket balls would scatter and hit many targets. No musket balls around? Soldiers filled the canisters with whatever was available: glass, nails, stones, even cutlery!

Weapons on Water

Ships were an important part of the War of 1812, since many battles took place on the Great Lakes, especially near Niagara Falls, and along the St. Lawrence River. Ships fired on forts and other ships, blockaded forts and moved soldiers and supplies.

Some ships were huge, heavy and studded with cannons — sometimes more than 100. These ships moved slowly but could do a lot of damage. Other ships were smaller with less firepower but could move in quickly to fire on an enemy vessel, then get out of range fast.

REBELLIONS OF 1837 AND 1838

By the late 1830s, rebellion had been brewing in Upper Canada (Ontario) and Lower Canada (Quebec) for years. People were tired of electing politicians who had little power. The real power was held by councils appointed by a governor chosen by Great Britain. In Upper Canada, critics called this group the Family Compact, since all the members seemed to be related. In Lower Canada it was known as the Château Clique. Many people felt it was time for change

A Peaceful Solution Fails

In Lower Canada, a group of young patriots called the Parti Patriote wrote down their demands for change in 1834. They called their document the "Ninety-two Resolutions."

Canada was governed by Britain in those days, so the demands were sent to London, England. The Patriotes waited for a response. And waited.

Finally, three years later, the British government sent back its answer. It rejected every one of the demands. Louis-Joseph Papineau, the Patriote leader, tried to calm the angry French Canadians, but other leaders, including Wolfred Nelson, called for rebellion.

St-Denis and St-Eustache

The rebels gathered in St-Denis, east of Montreal. Led by Nelson (Papineau had fled), they blocked the road and waited for the British troops. On November 23, 1837, the two sides met in a fierce battle. The British were forced to retreat.

Two days later, a second British force met the rebels at nearby St-Charles. The Patriotes were determined. But they were ordinary citizens with makeshift weapons, while the British soldiers had the latest in weaponry. The British won the battle, killing 150 Patriotes.

On December 14, the forces met again, this time at St-Eustache, near Montreal. The Patriotes had taken up position in the village church, so the British soldiers set it on fire. As the Patriotes raced out the doors and jumped from windows to escape the flames, the British shot them down. Their leader, Jean-Olivier Chénier, fought to the death.

The battle of St-Eustache

Back in York

Meanwhile, in Upper Canada, citizens were angry, too. They were sick of waiting for things they needed, such as bridges, roads and schools. After losing an election marked by bribery and threats, newspaper owner William Lyon Mackenzie called for rebellion.

On December 5, 1837, more than 600 rebels gathered in what is now north Toronto. They desperately wanted change but were armed only with clubs, pitchforks and some rifles. When they marched down Yonge Street, the main road, well-armed soldiers on the British side ambushed them. Mackenzie's rebels panicked and scattered. Two days later the British attacked the rebels and within half an hour had beaten them. But Mackenzie managed to escape.

"UP THEN, BRAVE CANADIANS! GET READY YOUR RIFLES, AND MAKE SHORT WORK OF IT!"

William Lyon Mackenzie

Canadian Courage

Louis-Joseph Papineau led the Lower Canada rebels. He was a skilled speaker who could inspire crowds to action. As the first important political leader of French Canada, he helped fight for French Canadian culture. But people had mixed feelings about Papineau. Some felt that he had deserted the Patriotes just before the fighting started.

The leader of the rebels in Upper Canada, William Lyon Mackenzie, was a hot-tempered newspaperman. He used his paper to demand political change. When Mackenzie got excited, he'd tear off his red wig and wave it around. To some he was a troublemaker, while to others he was a hero. York became the city of Toronto in 1834, and Mackenzie was its first mayor.

Louis-Joseph Papineau

William Lyon Mackenzie

Return of Mackenzie

After the failed rebellion of Upper Canada, William Lyon Mackenzie escaped to the United States, where he met up with a secret group that supported the Canadian rebels. At the end of December 1837, they helped Mackenzie get to Navy Island just above Niagara Falls, where he declared himself "President of the Canadian Republic."

British troops fired at Navy Island. They set Mackenzie's supply ship, the *Caroline*, on fire and sent it over Niagara Falls. Mackenzie had no choice but to flee to the United States again, where he was imprisoned for a year for the trouble he'd caused. More men died in these American-supported raids than in the original rebellion.

The Rebellions End

The French Canadian rebels hadn't given up either. In the United States, they banded together with the Frères Chasseurs (Hunters' Lodges), a group similar to the one that supported Mackenzie. They launched a number of attacks on the British troops in the Eastern Townships and around Montreal, but they were too disorganized to win.

Raids continued in Upper Canada as well. But by the beginning of December 1838, the rebellions were over. More than 1000 rebels had been captured, about 15 were hanged, and at least 800 were sent to prison. Others were exiled from Canada or sent as prisoners to Australia.

The government of Upper Canada believed William Lyon Mackenzie and his supporters were so dangerous that it offered rewards for their capture. But so many citizens supported the rebels that no one turned them in.

PROCLAMATION.

BY His Excellency SIR FRANCIS BOND HEAD, Baronet, Lieutenant Governor of Upper Canada, &c. &c.

To the Queen's Faithful Subjects in Upper Canada.

In a time of profound peace, while every one was quietly following his occupations, feeling secure under the protection of our Laws, a band of Rebels, instigated by a few malignant and disloyal men, has had the wickedness and audacity to assemble with Arms, and to attack and Murder the Queen's Subjects on the Highway—to Burn and Destroy their Property—to Rob the Public Mails—and to threaten to Plunder the Banks—and to Fire the City of Toronto.

Brave and Loyal People of Upper Canada, we have been long suffering from the acts and endeavours of concealed Traitors, but this is the first time that Rebellion has dared to show itself openly in the land, in the absence of invasion by any Foreign Enemy.

Let every man do his duty now, and it will be the last time that we or our children shall see our lives or properties endangered, or the Authority of our Gracious Queen insulted by such treacherous and ungrateful men. MILITIA-MEN OF UPPER CANADA, no Country has ever shewn a finer example of Loyalty and Spirit than YOU have given upon this sudden call of Duty. Young and old of all ranks, are flocking to the Standard of their Country. What has taken place will enable our Queen to know Her Friends from Her Enemies—a public enemy is never so dangerous as a concealed Traitor—and now my friends let us complete well what is begun—let us not return to our rest till Treason and Traitors are revealed to the light of day, and rendered harmless throughout the land.

Be vigilant, patient and active—leave punishment to the Laws—our first object is, to arrest and secure all those who have been guilty of Rebellion, Murder and Robbery.—And to aid us in this, a Reward is hereby offered of

One Thousand Pounds,

to any one who will apprehend, and deliver up to Justice, WILLIAM LYON MACKENZE; and FIVE HUNDRED POUNDS to any one who will apprehend, and deliver up to Justice, DAVID GIBSON—or SAMUEL LOUNT—or JESSE LLOYD—or SILAS FLETCHER—and the same reward and a free pardon will be given to any of their accomplices who will render this public service, except he or they shall have committed, in his own person, the crime of Murder or Arson.

And all, but the Leaders above-named, who have been seduced to join in this unnatural Rebellion, are hereby called to return to their duty to their Sovereign—to obey the Laws—and to live henceforward as good and faithful Subjects—and they will find the Government of their Queen as indulgent as it is just.

GOD SAVE THE QUEEN.

Monday, 3 o'clock, P. M. 7th Dec.

☞ The Party of Rebels, under their Chief Leaders, is wholly dispersed, and flying before the Loyal Malitia. The only thing that remains to be done, is to find them, and arrest them.

William Lyon Mackenzie's enemies called him William "Liar" Mackenzie. Mackenzie was the grandfather of Canada's tenth prime minister, William Lyon Mackenzie King (page 52).

Rebellion Results

In 1838, the British government sent Lord Durham (below) to Canada to find a way to bring peace to the colony. Durham spent little time in Lower Canada and decided that the French Canadians were backward and had little real history. He completely ignored their many accomplishments and rich culture. Instead, Durham decided French Canada should be absorbed by English Canada.

Durham thought that one way to end the rebellions and weaken French Canadian culture would be to unite the two Canadas. So in 1841, Upper Canada became known as Canada West, Lower Canada was renamed Canada East, and together the colony was called the Province of Canada.

Durham also suggested that the colony have "responsible government." That meant giving power to a single elected Assembly, made up of an equal number of members from both Canadas. Members of the Assembly included Mackenzie, Nelson and Papineau.

Other Battles

In the mid-1800s, some Canadian soldiers took part in the Crimean War, a conflict that took place between 1854 and 1856 in the Crimea, which is now part of Ukraine. Britain, France, Sardinia and Turkey fought Russia for control of the area.

No Canadian regiments or units were involved in this war, although some individual Canadian soldiers did fight in the British army. One of them, Alexander Roberts Dunn, became the first Canadian to earn the Victoria Cross (page 67), Britain's top prize for battle bravery.

All British troops stationed in Canada went to fight in the Crimean War. To replace them, Canada set up its own militia (an army made up of citizens rather than professional soldiers) in 1855.

Back at home, in the 1860s, Canadians were being threatened by Fenian raids. Fenians were Irish Americans who wanted to end British rule in Ireland. They also wanted to stop British rule in Canada.

Fenians attacked New Brunswick in April 1866, Ontario two months later and Quebec in 1870. They planned to raid Manitoba in 1871 but were stopped at the American border.

Although the Fenians were never a major threat, they frightened people. The raids were one of the events that convinced Canadians that they should unite into one country. In 1867, the Dominion of Canada was formed by New Brunswick, Nova Scotia, Ontario and Quebec, with more provinces joining in the years to come.

This ribbon was given to soldiers who fought the Fenians at the Battle of Ridgeway in June 1866 at Fort Erie, Ontario.

WE STAND ON GUARD

You can tour Mackenzie House in Toronto where William Lyon Mackenzie lived. Be sure to visit the print shop and museum. But beware — some people believe that this building is the most haunted house in all of Canada!

MÉTIS REBELLIONS

In 1867, Canada became a country made up of four provinces, all in the eastern half of the land. Prime Minister John A. Macdonald wanted to expand Canada from the Atlantic Ocean to the Pacific. That chance came in 1869, when the Hudson's Bay Company agreed to sell its vast territory in the north and the west.

But no one discussed the sale with the people who were living on the land. When the Métis (people of mixed European and First Nations descent) in the Red River area, around today's Winnipeg, heard about it, they decided they must act.

Measuring Mistake

Even before the land sale became final, many people from eastern Canada and the United States began moving into the Red River area. The Métis worried that they would lose their culture, their Catholic religion and their land.

In 1869, government surveyors began marking off land for settlers. They were supposed to survey only unoccupied land, but they began measuring Métis-owned land as well. In October 1869, the surveyors were stopped by a group of furious Métis and their leader, Louis Riel.

Red River Rebellion

Louis Riel was born in the Red River Settlement. The Métis chose him as their leader because he was well educated, as a priest and a lawyer.

After stopping the surveyors, Riel and his followers took over Upper Fort Garry, the main trading post on

Louis Riel (on horseback) united the Métis.

the Red River. They also set up a provisional (temporary) government to negotiate with the Canadian government.

Riel's provisional government wrote up a "List of Rights" to present to the prime minister. Its aim was to protect Métis land and customs. While the two sides were negotiating, a group of Canadians attacked, but ended up surrendering to the Métis.

Most of the Canadians were later released. But one of them, Thomas Scott, was considered by many Métis and Canadians to be an obnoxious troublemaker. The Métis tried and executed him in March 1870. Some people in Canada — especially those from Ontario, where Scott had lived — were angered by the execution and vowed revenge on Riel and his followers.

Manitoba

Prime Minister Macdonald agreed with almost all of the Métis demands. On July 15, 1870, the Hudson's Bay Company's land became Canada's, and the province of Manitoba was created. It included territory reserved for the Métis.

Riel is often called "the Father of Manitoba" because he'd been so involved in the province's creation. But he decided to flee his home on August 24, 1870, when government troops arrived. They'd been sent to reassure Ontario and help establish the new province. But Riel worried that he might be arrested so escaped to the United States.

Macdonald tried to persuade Riel to stay out of Canada, but instead Riel returned and entered federal politics. Between 1873 and 1874, he was elected to the House of Commons three times. But he was not allowed into the House because of his role in the execution of Scott.

Louis Riel (middle row, third from left) and his government council in 1870.

In Exile

Riel was banished from Canada for five years (1875–80). During those years he had a nervous breakdown and spent time in a mental institution. He also became obsessed with religion. In June 1884, Riel was working as a teacher in Montana when a group of Saskatchewan Métis asked him to return to Canada and help them stand up for their rights.

DID YOU KNOW

In the 1870s, the prairies were becoming lawless and dangerous. So the Canadian government created the North-West Mounted Police. In 1920, the force became known as the Royal Canadian Mounted Police. It still provides policing across Canada today and peacekeeping around the world.

Misery on the Prairies

As white settlers poured into Manitoba, they pushed the Métis west into Saskatchewan. There, the same thing happened — white people moved into the area. The Métis were once again afraid they would lose their land.

First Nations people were also fearful. The government had moved the Assiniboine, Blackfoot, Cree and Sioux people onto reserves and promised to provide them with food. But the promise was broken. To make matters worse, the buffalo that the First Nations people depended on for food and other necessities were being hunted almost to extinction by white hunters.

The Métis turned to Louis Riel to help. More fighting broke out when the North-West Mounted Police (NWMP) arrived. This time First Nations people were also involved.

North-West Rebellion

On March 18 and 19, 1885, Riel and the Métis set up another provisional government at Batoche, Saskatchewan. About a week later, the Métis and First Nations people fought the first of many battles against the NWMP.

After a fight at Fort Pitt in mid-April, 5000 government troops arrived. They far outnumbered the Métis and First Nations soldiers and were much better equipped. For instance, during the Battle of Batoche, the Métis ran short of ammunition. They dug enemy bullets out of walls to reuse them and even fired buttons, nails and rocks.

Riel was forced to surrender on May 15, 1885, after being defeated in the Battle of Batoche. The North-West Rebellion ended less than three weeks later.

What Happened When?
The North-West Rebellion set off many battles in what is now Saskatchewan during the spring of 1885.

March 26
Led by expert hunter Gabriel Dumont, the Métis fight the NWMP at Duck Lake (near Batoche) and win.

March 30
Starving First Nations people attack Battleford.

April 2
First Nations people battle the NWMP at Frog Lake (north of today's Lloydminster) and win.

April 15
The NWMP are beaten by First Nations people at Fort Pitt (near the Alberta border).

Riel's Legacy

Riel was tried in court and sentenced to death. Three times the execution was postponed, but finally he was hanged at Regina on November 16, 1885. Riel caused a huge divide among Canadians. People still argue about him. To some he's a hero because he defended the Métis and helped make Manitoba part of Canada. To others, Riel is a traitor because he started two rebellions.

The Herald. EXTRA.

PRICE 5 CTS.

Capture of Riel!

Government troops were brought in by train to put down the Métis rebellion.

Canadian Courage

Cree chief Poundmaker was a skilled speaker and peacekeeper. But when the government cut the food rations it had promised his people, he couldn't stop them from looting an abandoned village. Poundmaker never took part in the fighting that followed, but he was still found guilty of treason and put in jail.

Big Bear, a Plains Cree chief, tried to negotiate with the government for better treaty terms for his people, but the government answered by cutting off their food rations. He tried to prevent the fighting that ensued but was convicted of treason and imprisoned.

Poundmaker

Big Bear

DID YOU KNOW

Women accompanied military forces throughout Canada during the 1700s and 1800s. They sometimes fought but more often cooked, sewed, did laundry and took care of the sick. It wasn't until the North-West Rebellion that women, working as nurses, were given official recognition as part of the military force in the field.

WE STAND ON GUARD

The site where the Battle of Batoche took place in Saskatchewan is now Batoche National Historic Site. There you can find out more about the battle, as well as Métis life. Riel House in Winnipeg is where Louis Riel's body lay in state after his execution.

April 24
Métis hold their ground against government troops at Fish Creek, near Batoche.

May 2
First Nations win at Cut Knife Hill (near Battleford).

May 9–15
The Battle of Batoche between Métis and government soldiers ends with defeat for the Métis.

June 3
Cree fighters lose to NWMP soldiers at Loon Lake, near Fort Pitt. This is the last battle of the rebellion and the last battle fought in Canada.

SOUTH AFRICAN WAR

The end of the 1800s was a time of great progress for Canada. The Klondike Gold Rush lured waves of fortune seekers to the Yukon Territory, hoping to get rich quick. The country welcomed thousands of immigrants from Europe and Asia to the prairies. Great improvements in agriculture soon followed.

There was peace in Canada for the first time in many years. But wars still raged elsewhere in the world. When Britain got involved with a war over settlers' rights in faraway South Africa, Canada was asked to help.

To War or Not?

Canadians were divided over whether to take part in the South African, or Boer, War. (The Boers were people who had come to South Africa from Holland.) Most English Canadians wanted to fight with Britain. But French Canadian leader Henri Bourassa argued that Canada's soldiers should only participate in wars that threatened their own country. Fighting in the South African war, Bourassa warned, could commit Canada to support Britain in other wars. Most French Canadians agreed.

At first Canadian Prime Minister Wilfrid Laurier tried to keep Canada out of the fight. Eventually, he said that Canada wouldn't force anyone to fight in South Africa, but it would send volunteers.

About 8000 Canadians volunteered, and Britain agreed to pay their salaries. Some of these soldiers replaced British soldiers stationed in Halifax so they could take part in the war. Others went to South Africa to fight.

Canadian Courage

Sam Steele was one of the first officers of the North-West Mounted Police. After policing during the Klondike Gold Rush, he fought in the South African War.

Steele commanded Strathcona's Horse regiment of 600 horseback soldiers. Their main job was to scout out the enemy's position, and they did it well. But Steele disliked some of the regiment's other jobs, such as burning towns and moving people into concentration camps.

Steele returned from South Africa and again volunteered for war service when World War I (page 40) broke out in 1914. Although he was then 65, he was accepted and made a major-general. He was named Sir Sam Steele in 1918, just a year before he died. Canada's sixth-highest mountain, in the Yukon Territory, is named after this Canadian legend.

Canadians into Battle

The Canadian volunteers arrived in Cape Town, South Africa, at the end of November 1899. They spent two months in training — a first for Canadian soldiers. As training progressed, it became clear that the Canadians had a special talent for fighting off surprise attacks. This skill would prove to be useful in the battles with the Boers to come.

Paardeberg

The Battle of Paardeberg in February 1900 marked the first time large numbers of Canadian troops saw battle overseas. The battle lasted nine days and was the biggest, bloodiest fight of the whole war.

Toward the end of the battle, the Canadians tried to surprise the Boer forces by attacking before dawn. But the 4000 Boers soon had the raiders under heavy fire. The soldiers from Canada were told to retreat, but two companies from the Maritimes — each with only about 125 men — kept firing.

Finally, the exhausted Boers surrendered. The Canadians had won the battle. One of the British commanders remarked, "Canadian now stands for bravery, dash and courage."

DID YOU KNOW

Donald Smith negotiated with Louis Riel in 1869 to help end the Red River Rebellion (page 32). Sixteen years later, he'd invested so much money in Canada's first cross-country railway that he was given the honour of pounding in the track's last spike. When the South African War broke out, Smith — now known as 1st Baron Strathcona and Mount Royal — created and paid for Strathcona's Horse regiment, still one of Canada's most famous units.

These soldiers were wounded at Faber's Put, South Africa, on May 30, 1900. It was one of the fiercest battles involving Canadians during the Boer War.

Fighting Back

The British weren't used to some of the Boers' tactics, such as staging ambushes or dynamiting trains. But Canadians were especially good at fighting back and gained a reputation as tough, skilled soldiers.

It wasn't just the Boers the Canadians had to fight. Diseases were also a big enemy. With little chance to wash and so many men crowded together, soldiers faced the quick spread of illness. Many died painfully and needlessly.

Lorne Mulloy was blinded during battle in the Boer War. His hat shows how tough the fighting was — notice the bullet holes.

The War Continues

For more than two years, Canadian soldiers fought alongside the British and their allies. News of battles at Zand River, Mafeking, Lydengurg and Hart's River was reported in Canadian newspapers. At Leliefontein, 90 Canadians were assigned to protect retreating British soldiers. The Canadians managed to hold off several hundred Boers.

DEC. 1899.

DEC. 1900.

"FOR ME THE PAST HAS NO REGRETS."

TROOPER L.W.R. MULLOY.

End and Honours

In May 1902, Britain and its allies won the South African War. Two hundred and twenty-four Canadians had died, and 252 were wounded.

Four Canadians won Victoria Crosses (page 67), Britain's highest military award. These soldiers fought when wounded or when incredibly outnumbered. One rescued a wounded soldier, while others kept weapons out of the Boers' hands.

Another Canadian private was nominated twice for a Victoria Cross but never received the honour. On hearing this, Britain's Queen Victoria knit him a scarf!

New Relations

The South African War widened the divide between French and English Canada. English Canadians were proud of the victory. French Canadians continued to question their connection to Great Britain.

Another British war was coming soon. In only a few years, Canada, Britain and the entire globe would be involved in the worst fighting the world had ever known: World War I.

Robert Baden-Powell was the founder of the World Scout Movement. He was also a British officer during the South African War. He liked the hats that most Canadian soldiers wore during that war and so made the flat-brimmed style the official hat of the Boy Scouts.

Born into a wealthy, important family in 1862, Georgina Pope expected to live a life of leisure. But then her family lost its money. Pope became a nurse, even though, back then, nurses were considered servants who couldn't find other work.

Pope volunteered to serve in the South African War and was one of the first military nurses to go overseas. The conditions were horrible. Despite epidemics and shortages of food and medical supplies, Pope and the group of nurses she led saved many lives. In 1903, she became the first Canadian to be awarded the Royal Red Cross medal.

Soon Pope was made head of the Nursing Service for Canada's Army Medical Corps. She went on to train nurses for World War I and served in France during that war. Because of Pope, people began to think of nurses as skilled professionals.

The Military Grows Up

In its early days, Canada didn't have a trained army. Instead it had a "militia" — ordinary citizens who volunteered to fight or who were compelled to. They fought alongside professional soldiers, called "regulars," from France or Britain.

When British troops stationed in Canada left during the 1850s to fight in the Crimean War (page 31), a permanent Canadian militia was set up. Then in the late 1800s, Canada established regiments of professional soldiers. Their main job was training militia units, but they also fought during the Red River Rebellion (page 32) and South African War (page 36) alongside militia volunteers.

Both part-time and regular forces in Canada were known as militia until World War II. In the 1950s, the militia became the Reserve Force. This part-time group still supports regular Canadian army units today. The Canadian Forces was formed on February 1, 1968, when the Canadian Army, Royal Canadian Navy and Royal Canadian Air Force merged.

WORLD WAR I

It was triggered by the assassination of Archduke Francis Ferdinand of Austria–Hungary in June 1914. Conflicts had been raging in Europe, and this was the last straw. War broke out. On one side were the Central Powers: Austria–Hungary, Germany and Turkey. On the other side were the Allies: France, Russia, Great Britain and its commonwealth countries, including Canada. Later Italy, Japan and the United States joined the Allies.

Canadians thought the war would end quickly. But they had four long years of fighting ahead.

Ypres
One of Canada's early battles was on April 22, 1915, at Ypres in Belgium. This was the first time Germans used chlorine gas in battle. It spread in a

Gas mask

In towns across Canada, including Victoria, British Columbia (above), troops trained for battle.

yellow-green cloud, blinding and suffocating the French soldiers on the front lines. As the gassed men retreated, Canadians rushed in and held back the Germans.

Two days later, the Germans attacked Canadian soldiers with gas. The Canadians soaked their handkerchiefs with muddy water or urine and held them over their faces. Despite the Germans' heavy shelling, the Canadians managed to stop them.

The fighting continued at Ypres for months. More than 6000 Canadians died. Many were wounded before they even started fighting.

The Somme
The Battle of the Somme, a river in northern France, was one of the longest and bloodiest battles of World War I. It also established Canadian soldiers' reputation for courage and determination when leading an attack. As well, it marked the first time tanks were used on the battlefield.

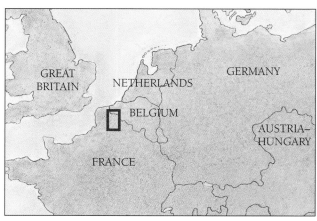

This map shows Europe before World War I. The main Canadian fighting happened in the red box.

Canadian troops leaving the trenches after the Battle of the Somme.

The battle started on July 1, 1916, and continued for three long months. As the Canadians prepared to attack the German-held town of Courcelette in September, Lieutenant-Colonel Louis-Thomas Tremblay wrote, "We know very well that we are heading to the slaughterhouse. The task seems nearly impossible, considering how ill-prepared we are."

Despite the constant barrage of bullets, the Canadians took the town and continued advancing — but slowly and at great human cost. More than 24 000 Canadians died during the Battle of the Somme.

Internment

In Canada, people were shocked by the number of soldiers being killed in the war. That made them distrust people living in Canada who had been born in enemy countries. So the government passed the War Measures Act.

The Act gave officials the right to arrest and imprison Austrians, Germans, Turks and Ukrainians. About 8600 innocent people were removed from their homes and forced to work in mines and logging camps for little or no money. It wasn't until 2005 that the Canadian government acknowledged this mistreatment.

Canadian Courage

Before World War I, Tom Longboat was one of the world's most famous athletes. This First Nations runner won countless marathons and broke many race records. Longboat quit racing to fight in the war. As a dispatch runner, he ran messages between groups of soldiers. Nothing could stop him, not even being wounded twice and once even being declared dead!

Beaumont Hamel

While most Canadians celebrate Canada Day on July 1, for many Newfoundlanders it is a time of great sadness. On that day in 1916, the Newfoundland Regiment suffered extreme losses.

The Allies' plan was to attack at the village of Beaumont Hamel on the Somme River, to break the Germans' front line. But the Germans were well prepared. Of the 801 members of the Newfoundland Regiment, only 68 escaped injury — the rest were killed, wounded or missing.

TECHNOLOGY OF WAR 3
TERROR FROM THE SKY

When Orville and Wilbur Wright flew the first airplane on December 17, 1903, they changed the way people travelled. But World War I brought another use for the airplane. The earliest warplanes were made of flimsy canvas and wood. At first they were used only to observe battles and scout out the enemy's position. But soon pilots were throwing objects such as bricks, grenades and ropes at enemy planes. Fliers also shot at opponents with guns and rifles.

Pilots wanted to mount guns on their planes to make the weapons easier to handle. But there was one big problem: the obvious place to position the gun was in front of the pilot. However, firing a gun mounted there would mean the pilot would be shooting at his own propeller.

The Germans solved the problem by linking the gun to the propeller with gears. The gun was timed to fire between the propeller's blades. The airplane became a dangerous weapon.

The Allies retaliated by capturing a German plane and copying its gun technology. That led to "dogfights" — battles in the air between two or more planes.

Fliers used cameras like this one to photograph the enemy's position.

"We had a scrap with a couple of [German] machines," remembered Canadian airman Basil Morris. "It was great shooting at the blighters and their machine-gun bullets were cracking all around us ... I didn't feel at all nervous up in the air during the scrap but was a bit shaky after we got back."

About 20 000 Canadians served with the Royal Flying Corps (it became the Royal Air Force toward the end of the war). That's a huge number considering the size of Canada's population. Canada provided more and better pilots to the Corps than any other country — more than 40 percent of all airmen fighting on the British side were Canadian.

Canadian Courage

Canadian airmen won their greatest fame as fighter pilots. Of the 27 top aces in the British Royal Air Force, ten were Canadians. They each had at least 30 victories and between them brought down more than 400 enemy aircraft.

Billy Bishop shot down 72 enemy planes, more than any other Canadian or British airman. In one battle, this ace brought down five planes in five minutes. He was the first flier from Canada to win the Victoria Cross (page 67). Bishop earned it for being the first flier ever to attack a ground force in enemy territory.

Second to Bishop with 60 victories was Ray Collishaw. In October 1916, he survived an attack by six German airplanes.

Billy Bishop

They shot out his instruments and partially blinded him, but Collishaw still managed to take down two of the enemy planes and make it to safety.

After shooting down a German plane, William Barker was attacked by about 60 more. He shot down three enemy aircraft before crash-landing. Over the course of the war, Barker brought down a total of 53 planes.

Other Canadian flying aces included Albert Desbrisay Carter, William Claxton, Donald MacLaren, Frederick R. McCall, Andrew McKeever, Francis Granger Quigley and J.L.M. White.

DID YOU KNOW

At the Great War Flying Museum in Cheltenham, Ontario, you can see airplanes from World War I, such as a Sopwith, Fokker and Nieuport, as well as uniforms and medals.

Ottawa is the home of the National Aviation Museum. Here you'll find planes from the past 100 years, including those used in peace and in war and from many different countries.

The Royal Canadian Air Force Memorial Museum in Trenton, Ontario, tells the story of Canada's Air Forces. Check out the planes, artifacts and equipment on display here.

Lieut. Blayney E. Scott Passes Away as Result of Wounds Received in Army.

Last week news of the death of Lieut. Blayney E. Scott, M. C., D. F. C., nephew of Blayney E. Maynard, Dr. S. C. Maynard and F. X. D. Maynard of San Jose, was received.

When the great war broke out Lieut. Scott was one of the first to enlist in the Canadian army, joining as a private, he soon won his commission by his bravery in the field. He received the military cross while serving with the French mortars, during the battle of Hill 70, he volunteered to carry messages between the batteries and the rear, when communication was cut off. To do this he had to pass through three dense barrages.

In 1917 he transferred from the artillery to the Royal Flying corps. While on a reconnoisance over the German lines, a piece of shrapnel tore a hole in the petrol tank. Realizing the danger, Lieut. Scott swung himself from his seat and crawled along the wing and stuffed a handkerchief into the hole but this not being sufficient, he returned to the cock-pit and stripped a piece of tin from the joy-stock, and with this and a piece torn from his cap, he was able to block the leak, thereby making it possible for the pilot to reach the British lines. For this act, he was awarded the distinguished flying cross.

Unfortunately in getting back to his seat he was thrown into the cock-pit and the head of the joy-stock struck him a heavy blow over the heart. He was invalided to England, but soon returned to France and was injured in another crash. As soon as he was able, he was back in the air service. He was severely wounded and sent again to England.

In February, the war being over he returned to Canada, where everything possible was done to restore him to health, but without success. Throughout his illness, his infectious humor and happy buoyant spirit never left him.

He was a model athlete, of splendid physique, in foeball, rowing, swimming and boxing, he carried off many honors.

In his death, Canada loses a gallant young officer and an athlete of unusual merit.

A host of friends, besides his relatives, will long mourn his loss.

Blayney Scott of Victoria, British Columbia, died on November 9, 1919. The highlighted section above describes how he was wounded. On page 45, you can see a letter he wrote to his uncle.

Vimy Ridge

The British and French had tried many times to take Vimy Ridge in Northern France but failed. In April 1917, it was Canada's turn to make an attempt.

The Canadians were well trained. They'd even been taught to use any German guns they captured. And they were using a new technology — Canadian colonel and scientist Andrew McNaughton had invented a way to locate German guns by their flare and noise so they could be quickly destroyed.

The attack on Vimy Ridge was scheduled to begin at dawn. That meant the soldiers had to lie out in the trenches all night. Falling drizzle chilled the men to the bone. Then, "At the arranged time, to the absolute second, suddenly, as dawn was breaking, every gun on the whole front opened up," remembered Lieutenant Claude Williams. "The roar of the heavy guns was deafening."

At Vimy, the British shelled the Germans, clearing the way for the advancing Canadians. Thirty thousand Canadians wrestled Vimy Ridge out of German hands. These brave soldiers gained more ground and captured more German guns and prisoners than in any previous Allied attack. It would be Canada's greatest victory of the war.

The man behind Canada's triumph at Vimy was Arthur Currie. General

"A BATTLE IS A GRAND THING WHEN YOU SEE PICTURES OF IT AND DESCRIPTIONS, BUT THEY ONLY SHOW UP THE BRIGHT SIDE OF THE AFFAIR ... WE SEE THE SHADY SIDE — THE HORRIBLY MANGLED DEAD, AND MUTILATED WOUNDED."

Lieutenant Claude Williams

The mud and blood of Passchendaele

Currie prepared carefully and was a strong leader. He was the first Canadian ever appointed to command all of Canada's ground combat forces.

Passchendaele

One of the war's most devastating battles took place on a marsh in Belgium. By October 1917, German and British soldiers had been fighting there for weeks. It had rained relentlessly, and the mud was waist deep at Passchendaele when the Canadians were ordered in. The mud swallowed soldiers, guns and supplies. Wounded men drowned in it.

For ten days the Canadians struggled to take Passchendaele from the Germans. It was a major victory, but almost 16 000 Canadians died in the fighting. And when it was over, "Here and there were bodies buried in the mud with only an arm or a leg showing above the surface," remembered soldier Arthur-Joseph Lapointe. "Everywhere I looked, all I could see was corpses covered in a shroud of mud."

Women Overseas and at Home

Canadian women weren't allowed to fight in World War I. But 5000 still found ways to serve, some for the Royal Air Force in Canada, others overseas driving ambulances and some as nurses.

Women also took over jobs in Canada so that the men could fight. More than 30 000 women worked in ammunition factories. Some knit or sewed, while others raised money for the war effort. All waited for those precious letters home from fathers, sons, brothers, husbands and sweethearts at the front.

Conscription

By 1917, Canada needed more soldiers. So Prime Minister Robert Borden proposed that Canada pass a conscription bill that made it mandatory for men to join the armed forces and fight.

When Parliament voted on conscription, the vote split along French–English lines. French members voted against it, arguing that this was a British war. The English felt it was the duty of Canadians to support their mother country, Britain. The French were outvoted, and conscription became the law.

DID YOU KNOW

Tanks were first used in World War I on September 15, 1916, halfway through the war. These tanks got stuck in the mud easily, and armour-piercing bullets could penetrate them. But tank technology improved, and little more than a year later, tanks were vital weapons.

ROYAL FLYING CORPS AUXILIARY HOSPITAL,

Over-seas Club Branch,

SHIRLEY PARK,
East Croydon.

Oct. 4th, Friday. 1918

Dear old Uncle 'Arry,

I sure was glad getting your letter 29th August, but when it comes to falling down on correspondence, I guess I am the guy. The girls will tell you that — between the three of them I guess I must owe them about fifteen letters. The fact is I don't deserve a gol darn letter. I know you've been having a pretty tough time with the old Jingle Pot and I sure am glad to hear you have got her started up again, and hope things will work smoothly from now on. In this country coal is going to be of more value than gold, pretty soon.

No doubt you've heard both Kay and I have been on the hospital list this last month. Kay was hit during the big Canadian advance on 16th Aug., Shrapnel through the left arm, but not at all serious. The wound has healed and although he hasn't regained full use of his arm, this will come in time with massage treatment, which he is getting at a convalescent camp just ten miles from here — Canadian Convalescent Campt, Epsom, Surrey. I went out to see him the other day and the only difference I could see, he seemed to be about a foot taller, I know I felt about as big as a minute alongside of him. I got mine about two weeks later, floating over the line one early morning on a low flying job, trying to locate Hun infantry during a push. We sure located them alright — the trouble was they happened to be shooting some-what straighter than usual that morning and put several bursts through the bus at about 500', at which height you don't stand much show with machine guns from the ground. They shot our old bus to pieces, but luckily didn't hit my pilot and only managed to get me with the last burst as we crossed the lines, diving, spinning and side-slipping "fanning the daisies" as the Kid calls it, with both our front and rear guns going full blast. The kid sure had them buffaloed to a fare-thee-well and it was one from the last lucky burst from the ground that got me through the back as I was stooping over to change a new drum. The kid kept his head all the time and about the next think I knew I was in a dressing station and they were cutting my clothes off. He sure is a wonder that kid and landed me 300 yds. from a Field Hospital. The fact that he did, making a perfect landing in a machine that was a "write off" was the one thing that saved my bacon, as I had already lost too much blood. However, by pumping me up with they soon brought we aroung-so that today, just about a month since I was hit, I am walking around in this Convalescent Home with nothing but a walking stick, having discarded my crutches last week.

Lieutenant Blayney Scott described being injured by the Hun (Germans).

"IN FLANDERS FIELDS"

The poem "In Flanders Fields" lifted soldiers' and civilians' spirits during the war. It also raised money for the war effort, became the war's best-known poem and is still recited around the world more than 90 years after it was written. Who wrote this famous poem? Canadian John McCrae.

McCrae was born in Guelph, Ontario, on November 30, 1872. He trained as a doctor but wrote poems and short stories in his spare time. When the South African War (page 36) broke out in 1899, McCrae postponed his studies to serve as a gunner.

Afterwards, McCrae studied and worked as a doctor in Canada and the United States. At the start of World War I, in 1914, he was among the first Canadians to sign up to go to Europe. McCrae was made a major and appointed brigade-surgeon to the First Brigade of the Canadian Forces Artillery. That meant he was responsible for a medical station at the front, in the midst of battle.

On April 22, 1915, McCrae began work at Ypres, in the area of Belgium known as Flanders. Although the Allies were holding firm, that date marked the first time the Germans used poison gas on their enemies.

Dead and injured men were rolled down into McCrae's dugout medical station. He worked long hours, only stopping to eat and sleep. There was no time for him to even change his clothes.

In Flanders Fields
—

In Flanders fields the poppies blow
Between the crosses, row on row,
That mark our place; and in the sky
The larks, still bravely singing, fly
Scarce heard amid the guns below.

We are the Dead. Short days ago
We lived, felt dawn, saw sunset glow,
Loved, and were loved, and now we lie
     In Flanders fields.

Take up our quarrel with the foe:
To you from failing hands we throw
The torch; be yours to hold it high.
If ye break faith with us who die
We shall not sleep, though poppies grow
     In Flanders fields

John McCrae
—

McCrae's famous poem in his own handwriting

On May 2, 1915, a close friend of McCrae's was shot and killed. "His diary's last words were, 'It has quieted a little and I shall try to get a good sleep,'" McCrae wrote. "His girl's picture had a hole right through it." After burying his friend, McCrae realized he couldn't help him or any of the dead soldiers, but he could try to make sure they were never forgotten. The next day, as the blood-red poppies waved over the battlefield around him, McCrae was inspired to write "In Flanders Fields."

The poem didn't seem very good to McCrae, and he threw it away. Luckily, another officer found it and sent it to magazines and newspapers in England. It was published on December 8, 1915, and was an immediate success. When it was used to encourage Canadians to buy Victory Bonds to support the war effort, $400 million came pouring in — almost three times the target amount.

McCrae continued caring for the wounded in France until January 1918, when he came down with

"*If ye break faith —
we shall not sleep*"

BUY VICTORY BONDS

pneumonia. Soon after, he also became ill with meningitis, a disease that causes high fever, headaches and severe nausea. On January 28, this soldier, doctor and poet died.

McCrae's poem was one of the main reasons why the poppy was chosen as a symbol to remember soldiers who have lost their lives fighting for their countries. Across Canada, Remembrance Day is celebrated each year at 11 a.m. on the

eleventh day of the eleventh month. November 11 is the anniversary of the armistice (agreement) that brought an end to World War 1 in 1918. Every year as the date approaches, war veterans with the Royal Canadian Legion sell poppies to raise money for veterans in need and their families.

"In Flanders Fields" was written about one battle from a long-ago war. But McCrae's poem still has meaning because it reminds us of the sacrifices soldiers make and the lives lost in war.

"WE ARE WEARY IN BODY AND WEARIER IN MIND. THE GENERAL IMPRESSION IN MY MIND IS ONE OF A NIGHTMARE."

John McCrae

WE STAND ON GUARD
The house in Guelph, Ontario, where John McCrae was born is now a museum. At McCrae House you can find information about this world-famous Canadian, see his war medals and more.

This World War I cemetery in Étaples, France, is just one of many in Europe.

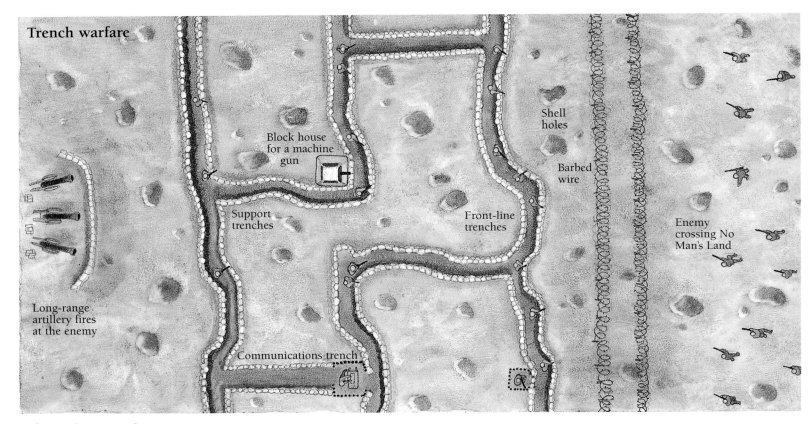

Trench warfare

Long-range artillery fires at the enemy

Support trenches

Block house for a machine gun

Communications trench

Front-line trenches

Barbed wire

Shell holes

Enemy crossing No Man's Land

Life in the Trenches

In September 1914, German soldiers in France dug trenches to protect them from advancing enemy troops. When the Allies realized they couldn't break this line of fortifications, they dug trenches, too. These trenches were zigzagging passages cut deep into the ground along the front of the battle lines. There the men would fight, eat and sleep for weeks.

Rain filled the trenches with cold, muddy water. "You should see us coming out of the trenches," said Lieutenant Claude Williams, "plastered from helmet to heel with [mud] inches thick, even our hands and face." Adding to the misery was

Soldiers in trenches could rest in "funk holes."

"EVERY STEP THAT I TOOK I WENT DOWN TO MY HIPS ... IT WAS A COMMUNICATIONS TRENCH FULL OF AUSTRALIAN DEAD BODIES. AND THEY HAD BEEN THERE FOR A MONTH OR SO, AND THE SMELL WAS SOMETHING."

Soldier George Hatch

a painful infection called trench foot, which soldiers got from standing in the muck.

Food was usually canned stew, corned beef or pork and beans. Bread was often mouldy by the time it reached the trenches. When no

supplies got through, soldiers went for days without food or water.

Even sleeping was tough in the trenches. In the cramped space, the men had to sleep fully dressed in case they were attacked. Their ammunition pressed on their chests,

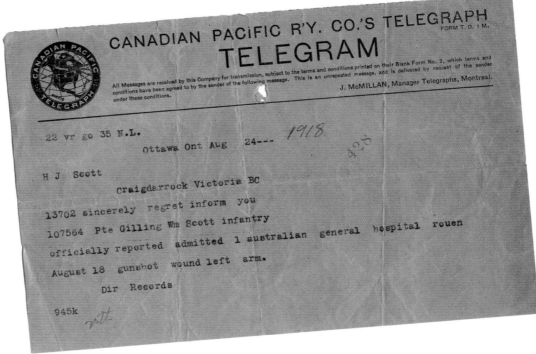

making it hard to breathe. Rats and lice crawled over them.

When reinforcements were sent in, weary soldiers had a few days off. During this break, they could visit a nearby town, eat a good meal and leave the horrors of war and the trenches behind for a little while.

Canada's Hundred Days

The last three months of World War I became known as the Hundred Days. Canadian soldiers had incredible successes on the battlefields, starting with the Battle of Amiens on August 8, 1918. There, Canadian and other Allied soldiers broke through the German lines and advanced 13 km (8 mi.) in one day. Canadians and their allies went on to attack enemy fortifications known as the Hindenburg Line and captured more than 30 000 soldiers.

The war was drawing to a close.

The parents of Private Gilling Scott received this telegram when he was wounded.

Germany finally surrendered, and World War I ended on November 11, 1918. This war became known as the Great War because it affected so many people. Some 625 000 Canadians had fought in the war. More than 61 000 had died and 154 300 had been wounded.

The Halifax Explosion

Halifax harbour was crowded with ships during World War I. On the morning of December 6, 1917, the Belgian ship *Imo* accidentally hit the *Mont Blanc* from France. The French ship was packed with explosives and blew sky high in the biggest man-made explosion up to that time.

Much of the north end of Halifax was destroyed by the blast, a tidal wave that followed and by fire. More than 1600 people died, and 9000 were injured. Charles Upham searched for his family's remains after the explosion: "We collected all that was left of my mother, my two sisters and my brother — some bones — and we put them into a shoe box …"

WE STAND ON GUARD

There are war memorials honouring Canadians throughout France and Belgium. Ottawa has two national monuments: the National War Memorial and the Memorial Chamber in the Peace Tower of the Parliament Building. Also in the Parliament Building is the Nursing Sisters' Memorial. Canadian sailors are remembered at Point Pleasant Park, Halifax, and Ross Bay Cemetery in Victoria, British Columbia.

WORLD WAR II

After World War I, it seemed impossible that Canada would go to war again. People's memories of the horrors were still too strong. But when German troops under their leader, Adolf Hitler, invaded Poland in 1939, that changed. Soon the battle lines were drawn. Germany was joined by such countries as Italy and Japan, and they became known as the Axis Powers. Fighting them were the Allies, including Britain, France, Australia, New Zealand, South Africa and Canada. (Russia and the United States would join later.) Canada was not automatically at war, as it had been when Britain joined World War I, but independently declared war on September 10, 1939.

Men who wanted to serve in the Canadian army had to fill in forms like this one.

"Phony War"

The first Canadian soldiers arrived in England in December 1939, ready to fight. But nothing much happened. People started calling it the Phony War because neither side launched any big attacks.

Then Germany invaded Denmark and Norway in April 1940 and France in May. Canadians landed in France in June 1940 ready to fight but were forced to retreat when the Germans took over France, Belgium and Holland.

Canada Takes to the Skies

One of Canada's biggest contributions to World War II was the British Commonwealth Air Training Plan (BCATP). This was a program to train aircrews from Australia, Canada, Great Britain and New Zealand, as well as the United States and occupied European countries. At its peak, there were 107 training schools and 184 other sites across Canada. When the program ended in 1945, it had produced more than 130 000 bombers, gunners, pilots, navigators and wireless operators.

Canada was the perfect place for the BCATP: it had wide-open skies, far from possible enemy attacks but close enough to Britain to be able to supply airmen quickly. You can find out more at the Commonwealth Air Training Plan Museum at the airport in Brandon, Manitoba.

The Battle of Britain

In the summer of 1940, Germany began attacking England — from the air. The Battle of Britain was the first battle in world history to be fought only with planes. There were only a few hundred Allied fighter pilots at that time and about 100 of them were Canadian. But some of the Canadians had never even fired at a moving target.

"It is certainly an awful sight to behold those ugly black bombers," remembered Canadian pilot Ernest McNab. "We fought far above the clouds in a world of our own — a world of freezing cold, of limitless space traced with white plumed trails of wheeling aircraft as they fought." By the end of October 1940, 23 Canadian pilots had given their lives to stop the Germans.

Pilot Ben Swenson's airforce cap

Battle of the Atlantic

Throughout the war, German submarines, called U-boats, attacked ships bringing supplies and aircraft to Britain from North America. Canadian corvettes (escort ships) and aircraft, based out of Newfoundland and the Maritimes, protected the supply ships.

"I cannot imagine a more miserable existence than this of being caught on a corvette in the Atlantic," said sailor Frank Curry. "An Atlantic so rough that it seems impossible that we can continue to take this unending pounding and still remain in one piece."

By the time the war ended, more than 25 000 supply ships would cross the Atlantic safely. The Royal Canadian Navy and Royal Canadian Air Force would sink 47 of the 790 enemy submarines destroyed by the Allies. About 2000 Canadians in the navy and 1600 in the merchant marines (other ships that helped the navy) would die trying to protect Allied ships.

Canadian ships escorted supply ships to protect them from German attack.

Hong Kong

World War II didn't take place just in Europe. In December 1941, Japan bombed Pearl Harbor, Hawaii, which brought the United States into the war. Then Japan began attacking throughout Southeast Asia. Soon the Japanese were targeting Hong Kong and Singapore, which then belonged to Britain.

Almost 2000 inexperienced Canadians, along with British and Indian soldiers, were sent to defend Hong Kong. They took on the tough Japanese army in mid-December 1941 but on Christmas Day had to surrender. More than 550 Canadians were killed or died in cruel prisoner-of-war camps.

Back at Home

Conscription became an issue in this world war just as it had in the last (page 45). Prime Minister William Lyon Mackenzie King didn't want to make conscription law because it was unpopular and might cost him the next election. So in 1942 he held a vote on whether Canadians would accept conscription. As in World War I, Quebec mostly voted no, while the rest of Canada mainly voted yes. But conscription was still too unpopular. King didn't introduce it until late in the war, in 1944.

King had other problems, too. On May 12, 1942, German submarines blew up two ships in the Gulf of St. Lawrence. There were many places along the coast for submarines to hide, and by November the Germans had sunk 18 ships. Canada had to improve its defences, and quickly.

Canadian soldiers on duty in Hong Kong

Internment

During the war, the government imprisoned Canadians of German, Italian and Japanese descent because they were thought to be a threat. Japanese Canadians were treated the worst. By September 1942, about 21 000 Japanese Canadians in British Columbia had had their homes and businesses taken away from them. Many were forced into internment camps.

When the war ended, Japanese Canadians were never paid back for all that had been taken from them. It wasn't until 1988 that the Canadian government finally apologized. Two years later the government apologized to Italian Canadians.

LICK THEM *over there!*

COME ON CANADA !

Canadian Courage

George "Buzz" Beurling was one of the top ten Allied fighter pilots of the war. During the 1942 battle for the island of Malta in the Mediterranean, he shot down 27 enemy airplanes in just two weeks.

Royal Canadian Air Force officer J.E. "Johnny" Fauquier won a top award, the Distinguished Service Order (DSO), for courage in 1943. By the end of the war he had received two more DSOs. He was the only Canadian airman to receive such high honours.

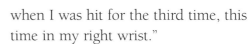

This War Medal 1939–1945 was awarded to Robert La Verne Armstrong of Ontario.

Dieppe

By 1942, the war was going badly for the Allies. The Germans occupied France, and German soldiers were also forcing their way into Russia. To test the German defences and take pressure off Russia, the British decided to attack Dieppe, a French coastal town held by the Germans.

It was a huge attack, involving at least 6000 Allies. And it was a nightmare. The Germans learned of the surprise attack ahead of time. They were ready for the soldiers who disembarked from ships on the beach at Dieppe. The Germans took aim at the Allied soldiers and mowed them down — an easy feat, since the raid occurred in broad daylight. The Allied tanks were useless — the beach was covered with large rocks. On all sides, the Germans kept firing.

"I think that I must have made no more than three steps before I was hit by a bullet for the first time and knocked to the ground," remembered Lieutenant-Colonel Dollard Menard later. "At first you don't feel the pain. I was hit a second time. The bullet hit me in the cheek and tore my face pretty badly. I managed to get up when I was hit for the third time, this time in my right wrist."

About 5000 Canadians were part of the attack on Dieppe — 3400 were captured, wounded or killed. People still argue about why the raid ended in such disaster. The next time the Allies attacked France's coast, they would not make the same mistakes.

More than 900 Canadian soldiers died at Dieppe on August 19, 1942.

TECHNOLOGY OF WAR 4
SPIES

Movies and books make spying look glamorous and exciting. The truth, especially during World War II, was another story. Spying was lonely, difficult work. Spies never knew whom to trust or what was around the next corner.

Canadian spies in World War II served with two British secret organizations: the Special Operations Executive (SOE) and MI-9 (Military Intelligence).

SOE agents fought the enemy from within enemy-occupied countries. They ambushed troops, disrupted communication and transportation and sabotaged German camps. They also taught these skills to people within the occupied countries.

MI-9 agents learned to parachute — usually at night — into enemy territory, kill silently and handle explosives. They also assisted prisoners of war and airmen shot down over enemy-held areas, helping them escape to safe territory.

Spies had to be on the alert at all times. If a secret agent was pretending to be a French labourer, a small detail such as wearing a North American watch or whistling a Canadian tune could give him away instantly. A German soldier trying to expose a spy would suddenly slip an English phrase or question into conversation, and the secret agent would have to pretend not to understand. A spy could never relax because it could mean death.

Most Canadian secret agents came from three groups: French Canadians, people from Italy and Eastern Europe and Chinese Canadians. French Canadians mostly served in France, since they already spoke the language — although they had to guard against using any Canadian expressions. After the raid on German forces in Dieppe, France, in August 1942, almost 1000 Canadian soldiers were taken prisoner, and Canadian spies helped some escape.

Canadian secret agents with European backgrounds parachuted into Hungary, Italy and Yugoslavia. Chinese Canadians served in Asia. In Europe, there were secret resistance movements organized by locals who helped the spies. But in Asia, spies were on their own.

For spies, the risk of being captured was huge, and they knew what to expect if caught: brutal interrogation, torture, starvation and probably death.

Canadian spies were incredibly brave men and women. They received no recognition for their work until many years after the war, when it was finally safe to identify them.

The True North

Spies weren't the only ones with secrets. Some Royal Canadian Air Force fliers also had a few tricks up their sleeves — or sewn to their jackets. They were given a button that looked like every other button on their uniforms, but the top could be twisted off to reveal a compass inside.

The airman replaced one of his regular buttons with this special one. Then if he had to bail out of the plane and didn't know where he was, he could consult his secret compass to find out which direction to walk.

Parachuting at night was dangerous. Spies couldn't see where they were landing and risked being shot at.

Canadian Courage

One of the most famous spies of World War II was Canadian William Stephenson. Born in Winnipeg in 1896, this master spy only had a Grade 6 education. But he was a millionaire before he was 30 thanks to a radio company he created in England and his invention of the wirephoto. This device made it possible to send photos over long distances without using wires.

While in England, Stephenson became friends with British prime minister Sir Winston Churchill.

When World War II started, Churchill asked Stephenson to run a spy network based in New York. The telegraph address was Intrepid, and that became Stephenson's code name.

Intrepid and his spies, some of them young Canadian women, figured out enemy codes, forged documents and sabotaged German atomic experiments. This master spy also trained agents at Camp X, a secret spy school near Whitby, Ontario, and helped maintain Hydra, a vital communications

centre located there. Some people say Stephenson was one of the most important people in the battle to defeat Hitler.

Italy

When the Allies invaded Sicily, Italy, in 1943, Canadians were there. They fought over incredibly rough countryside, earning a reputation for toughness. The battle took 38 days, but the Allies eventually won a base for moving farther into Italy.

In miserable winter weather in Ortona or summer heat in Rimini, the Canadians battled through machine guns and land mines and kept advancing. About 93 000 Canadians served in Italy, and 5400 lost their lives.

Escape

The war's most daring escape depended on Canadian Wally Floody. He was an airman who was taken to a German prison camp, where he discovered the prisoners were planning to tunnel to freedom. Floody was a miner, so he became the "Tunnel King," responsible for planning the tunnel.

On March 24, 1944, 76 prisoners escaped. Floody wasn't one of them — he'd been sent to another camp. To find out more, watch the movie *The Great Escape* — the character Danny is based on him.

D-Day

The Allies had learned their lesson at Dieppe. For their next European invasion, they spent months training soldiers and planning.

Just after midnight on June 6, 1944, the day ever after known as D-Day, Allied airplanes and ships began bombarding the Germans stationed on the north coast of France, in the region of Normandy.

"The moon played hide and seek with the clouds and we expected any moment to be the target for shore batteries," said soldier Frank Curry later. "[Royal Air Force was] blasting

On D-Day, soldiers waded from troop-carrier ships up onto the beach.

away all along the coast, so close that we could feel the jar of the bombs continuously. Great fires started all along and over 50 planes came down in flames throughout the long and terrible night."

Robert La Verne Armstrong earned the France and Germany Star for service during the last year of World War II.

During World War I, most Black Canadian soldiers had had to fight in segregated units. But in World War II, they fought alongside white soldiers in mixed regiments. Seven sons in the Carty family of Saint John, New Brunswick, served in the war. Adolphus, Clyde, Donald, Gerald and William all joined the air force, while Malcolm and Robert fought with the army in Europe and the Middle East. They all survived the war and returned home to Canada.

At dawn, more than 100 000 soldiers — including 15 000 Canadians — began pouring out of troop-carrier ships. Canadians landed on the beach between Vaux and St Aubin-sur-Mer — an area code-named Juno Beach. They had to cross the open beach under heavy German machine gun and mortar fire.

"We had never felt so alone in our lives," says Charlie Martin, a sergeant major, about landing on the beach.

"Everything was dead quiet. Except at any second we were expecting the German shelling to start. And it did."

Those who made it ashore ended up fighting in the streets of the nearby French towns. Some Canadians faced special units of German soldiers known for their ruthlessness. But by the end of D-Day, Canadians had advanced 9 km (6 mi.) inland — more than any other Allied soldiers.

However, the victory cost 340 Canadians their lives. As well, another 574 were wounded and 47 were taken prisoner. "Half of our original company — those I had joined up with in June 1940 — had been killed or wounded," remembers Martin. "The tears came … So many had been taken."

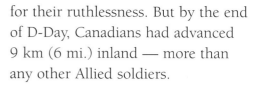

DID YOU KNOW

June 6, 1944, wasn't the first time the term D-Day was used by the military. It had long been used to indicate the first day of an attack when the actual date hadn't been decided or had to be kept secret. The Normandy invasion was so important that the term D-Day became forever associated with it.

Canadian soldiers (standing, left) guarding German prisoners (sitting).

Normandy Invasion

Despite fierce fighting, the Canadians continued to penetrate into France, helped by Allied airplanes. Throughout June and July of 1944, the fighting went on. At Caen, the Canadians fought a German unit notorious for its cruelty but still captured the city.

Canadian soldiers pushed on and in August took the French town of Falaise. Major David Currie said: "In the distance we could see rising clouds of dust. We were witnessing the remnants of the German forces in France trying to escape … The column stretched as far as we could see. It was an awe-inspiring sight."

A Canadian artillery officer remembers, "It was as if the

This bridge over the Orne River in France was seized by Canadians in June 1944.

Bomber Command

Some Royal Canadian Air Force fliers were assigned to Bomber Command. It had the dangerous job of dropping bombs deep inside German territory. "We also did a number of what were known as mining raids, where we dropped mines in harbours so that the harbour would not be available to the German fleet," remembered RCAF navigator Rae MacLeod (third from left).

Bomber Command planes had to cross the intimidating German anti-aircraft defence of guns and mortars. Almost 10 000 Canadians lost their lives in this perilous work.

Americans and British were huge brooms sweeping the Germans into the dustpan which at that moment was the Canadian Army." Soon the Allies were chasing the Germans into Belgium and the Netherlands.

The Normandy Invasion was the largest invasion by sea in the world's history — more than 3 million troops took part. About 18 500 Canadians were killed or wounded during the three-month-long campaign that marked the beginning of the end for the German forces.

Canadian soldiers didn't just fight — they also helped the victims of the war.

Quebec Conferences

Meanwhile, back in Canada, the Allied leaders were discussing strategy. They met in Quebec in August 1943 and September 1944. Canada's Prime Minister King hosted Winston Churchill, Great Britain's prime minister; Franklin Delano Roosevelt, president of the United States; and Josef Stalin, Russia's leader. King didn't join the sessions — lots of other countries would then have wanted to as well — but many feel he played an important role in helping the leaders get along.

Into Belgium

Canadians moved along the Atlantic coast, crushing German strongholds as they went. In early October 1944, they fought to gain control of the Scheldt River in Belgium. The area was wet and swampy, and Canadian soldiers were often slogging through mud up to their waists.

It took a month of heavy fighting, but by November 8 the Canadians had taken over the Scheldt. This was an important victory because it allowed the Allies to send badly needed supplies up the river. But it killed or wounded more than 6300 Canadians.

Women at War

About 45 000 Canadian women enlisted in World War II. Approximately 5000 went overseas and saw duty in the Women's Royal Canadian Naval Service, the Canadian Women's Army Corps and the Royal Canadian Air Force (Women's Division). Canadian women weren't allowed to fight but instead held jobs such as drivers, mechanics and radar operators.

In Canada, at least 261 000 women built guns, aircraft and other equipment. The head of Canada's airplane production was engineer Elsie MacGill (left).

Women who didn't serve during the war or work in war-related industries still made major contributions. They knitted, prepared bandages, wrote letters to soldiers and collected scrap — bones, fat, metal and rubber could all be made into ammunition and tanks. Although food was rationed, women fed their families well: it was a Canadian's duty to eat a healthy diet.

Women also collected money for the war through Victory Bond drives, which raised $12.5 million. Kids bought war savings stamps to help out.

Kay (Cattanach) Black served in the Canadian Women's Army Corps and was stationed in England and Holland.

DID YOU KNOW

Imagine sailing to a country you've never seen, to live with a husband you hardly know. That's what 43 500 "war brides" did during and after World War II. These adventurous women, mostly British, were shocked by their new country's size and weather. But most stayed and learned to call Canada home.

Canadians Free Holland

The Allies kept advancing across Europe. Canadians helped push the Germans east through the Netherlands (Holland) across the Rhine River, fighting across plains and through forests. British and American troops continued the advance, while Canadians were sent to northern Holland.

As Hitler saw his empire crumbling around him, he committed suicide on April 30, 1945. Germany surrendered to the Allies. May 8 became known as VE Day — "VE" stands for "Victory in Europe."

Canadian troops ended the war in Holland. They brought food, supplies and, most importantly, freedom to the cold, starving people. "When the Canadian troops came, people started running out of their houses with flowers and climbed on the tanks," said Lini Grol, who was a young woman at the time. "Everybody was so happy and started crying, including me: it was the most beautiful day of my life."

On VE Day, a Royal Canadian Navy officer saw something he hadn't seen in years. "The sight of 60-odd ships — well formed into convoy and fully illuminated — was a truly remarkable one, and after five-and-a-half years of darkness, a little frightening to behold."

How did most Canadian soldiers celebrate the end of the war? By collapsing with exhaustion. Many had seen heavy combat for days and could finally rest.

Canadian soldiers and the people of Holland celebrate the end of the war.

Canadians celebrated in the streets when they heard the news that World War II was over.

The War Finally Ends

The war in Japan continued but would soon come to a sudden end. The United States now had devastating atomic bombs — made from Canadian uranium. On August 6, a bomb was dropped on Hiroshima, one of the country's major cities, then three days later another on Nagasaki.

About 150 000 adults and children died within days or over the next year, while those who lived suffered from horrible radiation burns and sickness. Victory in Japan, or VJ Day, took place on August 14, 1945, when Japan surrendered. World War II was finally over.

The Albertan

WORLD WAR OVER

MacArthur to Accept Formal Japanese Surrender
Wednesday Declared National Holiday for Dominion

Blankets World
As Allied Leaders
Order 'Cease Fire'

Allies Accepted Terms
But Never Saw Jap Note

'V-J Day'
Declared

Petain Found Guilty,

Canada's Record

During World War II, more than 1 million men and women joined Canada's armed forces. Canadians served in Europe, the Mediterranean, the Middle East, North Africa, the Pacific and Southeast Asia. It was an incredible contribution coming from a population of only 12 million.

At least 42 000 Canadians lost their lives during the war, and 55 000 were wounded. It was a high cost for Canada and its citizens, but an enemy as dangerous as Hitler had to be stopped. Canada's fighting forces gained high respect from their allies and enemies.

WE STAND ON GUARD

There are many sites in Canada that commemorate Canadians' contributions to WWII, including:

- Fort Rodd Hill, in Victoria, British Columbia
- HMCS *Sackville*, in Halifax harbour, near Pier 21 immigration museum
- North Atlantic Aviation Museum in Gander, Newfoundland
- RCAF Memorial Museum in Trenton, Ontario

All of these have Web sites where you can find out more.

The tulip bulbs that bloom in Ottawa every spring are a thank-you from the Dutch royal family — during the war, some of them fled to Ottawa.

The Holocaust

During World War II, more than 6 million Jewish people died at the hands of Adolf Hitler and his followers, the Nazis. He believed that Jews were an inferior race and so should be eliminated.

Starting in 1940, Jews were sent to concentration camps, where they were tortured, starved, shot or gassed to death. When the war ended in Europe in May 1945, the death camps were liberated, and for the first time people discovered just how terribly the Jews had been treated. "I felt as if I were in another world," said Canadian journalist René Lévesque. "What we discovered was anti-Semitism [prejudice against Jews], but above all it showed where the descent into barbarism can lead."

The surviving Jews again faced discrimination when they tried to leave Europe. Canada made it very difficult for them to immigrate to our country and accepted fewer than 5000 Jews, a far smaller number than similar nations.

KOREAN WAR

By the end of World War II, Canada was one of the world's richest countries. Oil, mining and forestry industries were all booming. There were lots of jobs, even for the many people who immigrated from European countries destroyed by the war.

Canada now had the world's third-largest navy and the fourth-largest air force. However, after experiencing the horrors of the two world wars, it seemed impossible that Canada would go to war again soon.

The United Nations Steps In

After World War II, the Asian country of Korea didn't have a government. It broke into two parts: North Korea backed by the Soviet Union (now Russia) and South Korea backed by the Americans. When North Koreans invaded the South on June 25, 1950, the United Nations (see box on page 63) ordered them to get out. But the North Koreans refused to leave, so the United Nations (UN) decided to send in troops. About 90 percent of these forces were American, but thousands of Canadians went as well.

Canadian soldiers on patrol in Korea.

By Land, Sea and Air

Canadian soldiers fought North Korean troops, bravely defending strategic positions, even when they were vastly outnumbered. They patrolled dense jungle, scouting out the enemy's position and ambushing enemy troops. During storms, patrols had to be careful not to be cut off from the rest of their company. "When it rained in Korea, a small trickling creek could become a raging river in a few hours," remembered soldier "Baj" Franklin.

Eight ships of the Royal Canadian Navy defended South Korean coastal villages. And a transport squadron of the Royal Canadian Air Force flew 600 round trips over the Pacific, carrying soldiers and supplies. Other Canadian pilots destroyed or damaged 20 North Korean jet fighters.

Kapyong and Koje-Do

Canadian fighters are especially remembered for their bravery in two battles. On April 24, 1951, Canadian soldiers fought all night to hold back the North Koreans in the Kapyong (now Gapyong) River Valley, an important route for moving troops.

Don Hibbs was in the midst of the battle. "There's people dying on both sides, you can hear them," he recalled years later. "It was terrifying, but also you resolved the fact that

you're there, there's no place to go, do the best job you can and do all the firing and all the fighting you can until you can't do it any more." Canadians inflicted heavy casualties on the enemy, without losing many of their own soldiers.

In May 1952, Canadians were called to the island of Koje-Do, where huge compounds held 160 000 North Korean prisoners who had taken over the camp. The Canadians managed to restore order.

Divided Still

A ceasefire was finally negotiated, and the Korean War came to an end in 1953. As Canadian Private D.A. Strickland remembered, "Months of pent-up emotions were released and loud shouting echoed across the valleys … We unloaded our weapons … and settled down for our first night's sleep in many weeks."

Of the 25 500 Canadians who served in the war, about 1200 were wounded and more than 300 were killed.

Korea is located between China and Japan.

Canada made a larger contribution in relation to its population than most other countries.

Korea continues to be divided. Troops from both sides still stand watch on either side of the zone that separates the two countries.

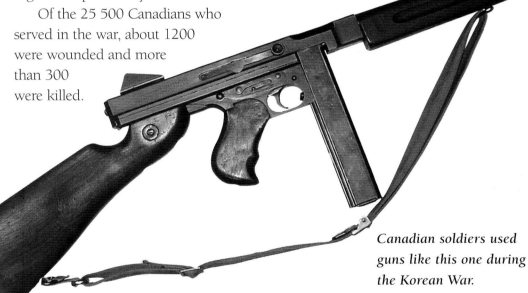

Canadian soldiers used guns like this one during the Korean War.

The United Nations

For many years, countries had been looking for an organization to help solve arguments between them. Even before World War II ended, people began working to establish the United Nations (UN). In 1945, 50 countries, including Canada, joined together to decide what the new organization would do. One of the UN's biggest roles is peacekeeping, and Canada has been very involved in this effort (see pages 64–67).

PEACEKEEPING AND MORE

In 1956, Canada created a new role for UN member countries. The man responsible was a Canadian diplomat (and later prime minister), Lester B. Pearson. He proposed sending UN troops to act as peacekeepers in areas where war and violence had broken out. Canadian troops were among the first UN peacekeepers, and they continue to play an important part in peacekeeping missions today.

The Suez Crisis

Countries worried they were on the brink of World War III in 1956 when Egypt suddenly took over the Suez Canal. The canal was located in Egypt but run by a French and British company, and the company wanted the canal back. Egypt refused, and on October 31, Britain and France bombed the area.

Lester Pearson (above) suggested to the United Nations that it create an emergency force to supervise a ceasefire between the two sides. His idea led to the first international peacekeeping unit, under the command of another Canadian, General E.L.M. Burns.

Pearson had brought the world back from the edge of war, and the next year he won the Nobel Peace Prize, one of the world's most famous awards. He is the only Canadian ever to win this prize. Lester Pearson went on to become Canada's prime minister in 1963.

Blue Berets

United Nations' peacekeepers wear distinctive pale blue berets so that they're easily recognizable. These hats have earned them the nickname the Blue Berets.

Blue Berets don't enter conflict zones unless both sides agree to have them — and to stop fighting. It's the peacekeepers' job to maintain the peace.

Peacekeepers don't take sides. Instead, they try to get the two sides working together to build a lasting peace. They aren't allowed to use their weapons unless they are directly attacked. They're not police, they're diplomats, and their best weapons are words, not guns.

> "WE NEED ACTION NOT ONLY TO END THE FIGHTING BUT TO MAKE THE PEACE ... MY OWN GOVERNMENT WOULD BE GLAD TO RECOMMEND CANADIAN PARTICIPATION IN SUCH A UNITED NATIONS FORCE, A TRULY INTERNATIONAL PEACE AND POLICE FORCE."
>
> *Lester Pearson*

Canadian peacekeepers patrolling in Cyprus.

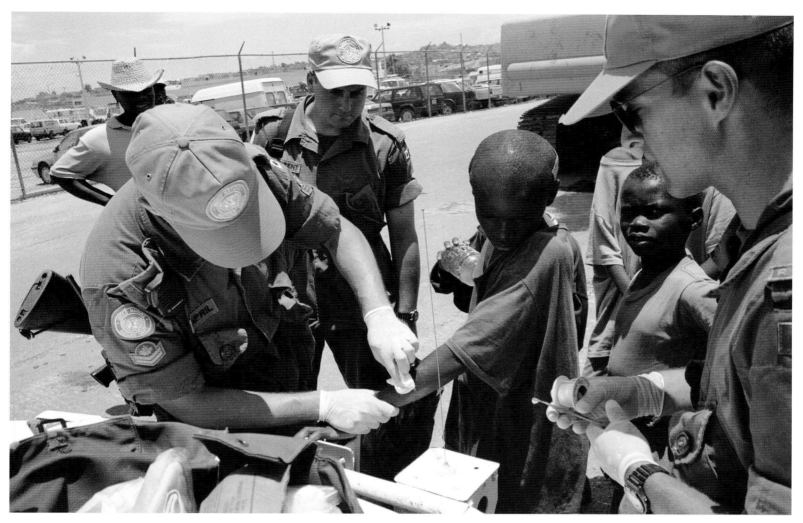

Canadian soldiers help with UN peacekeeping missions in many countries. Here one helps an injured boy in Port-au-Prince, Haiti.

Canadians have been part of every major UN peacekeeping mission since the first one to Egypt in 1956. They've served in the Congo (1960), Cyprus (1964), Somalia (early 1990s), Bosnia-Herzegovina (2000s), Sudan (2004) and many other countries.

NATO and NORAD

The Suez Crisis reminded Canada and the world how easy it would be for a major war to break out. In 1949, Canada had become a member of the North Atlantic Treaty Organization (NATO), a group of ten European countries plus the United States, that promised to work together if any of their countries were attacked. (There are now 16 countries in NATO.)

In 1958, Canada joined the United States to create the North American Aerospace Defence Command (NORAD). Today it uses aircraft, radar and satellites to watch for missile attacks in the skies over North America.

WE STAND ON GUARD

During the 1950s and 1960s, many Canadians feared their country might face a nuclear attack. So a secret, heavily protected bunker was built outside Ottawa for government use in case of emergency. When the bunker opened in 1961, the prime minister was John Diefenbaker, so it was nicknamed the Diefenbunker. Today you can tour the underground building and find out about life in the 1960s.

Canadian Courage

By the time Lewis MacKenzie retired from the Canadian forces in 1993, he'd achieved the rank of brigadier-general. He'd earned it — MacKenzie had served in peacekeeping operations around the world. He visited such war-torn countries as Cyprus, Vietnam, Egypt and the Gaza Strip in the Middle East. MacKenzie was commander of a UN Observer Mission to Central America in 1990 and chief of staff for the UN Protection Force in Yugoslavia in 1992.

Troubles at Home

In the 1960s, tensions were growing in Quebec. Some Quebecers wanted to be independent from Canada. A group called the Front de libération du Québec (FLQ) began setting off bombs in Montreal. Their terrorist actions killed six people and injured at least 40.

When the FLQ kidnapped a British diplomat and a Quebec politician in October 1970, Canadians were outraged. Prime Minister Pierre Trudeau sent in armed troops to help the police. He also used the War Measures Act to extend the power of the government and give police the right to arrest people without explanation.

The "October Crisis" was the first time the Act had been used in peace-time. The members of the FLQ were eventually captured, but not before murdering one of their hostages.

Canada's army was called in again in 1990, when Mohawks in Oka, near Montreal, barricaded woods that were scheduled to be cut down. A standoff between soldiers and protesters lasted for months, and before it ended, a police officer was killed.

Massacre in Rwanda

Sometimes there's nothing peacekeepers can do when violence explodes. When Canadian General Roméo Dallaire (right) was head of a UN Peacekeeping Force in Rwanda (in central Africa) during 1994, he didn't have enough peacekeepers to stop a horrible massacre. Hundreds of thousands of Rwandans died, and all Dallaire and his staff could do was watch in horror. In 1999, the United Nations acknowledged its failure to act and accepted blame for this terrible incident.

In Afghanistan, a Canadian soldier keeps watch as his convoy takes a break.

Dallaire continues to speak out about what happened in Rwanda so that no one will forget and so that it will never happen again. He is now trying to help children who are affected by war, including children forced to be slaves and soldiers.

Overseas Action

When Iraq invaded Kuwait in August 1990, the UN authorized the use of force to drive out the Iraqi soldiers. The resulting conflict became known as the Gulf War. With the United States leading the attack, Canada sent in 2400 soldiers, as well as ships, airplanes and supplies and medical staff. No Canadians were killed during the fighting.

In 2001, the United States led another attack, this time against Afghanistan. Once again Canada joined them. Afghanistan was sheltering terrorists, so Canada sent in troops. Thousands of Canadians have seen duty in Afghanistan. Many have been killed and wounded as they struggle to bring peace and security to the country, as well as help reconstruct roads, schools and more.

The Victoria Cross

The Victoria Cross is the British Commonwealth's highest award for military bravery. It got its name from Britain's Queen Victoria, who created the award in 1856. The first Canadian to ever win it was Alexander Roberts Dunn, who was rewarded for courage in the Crimean War (page 31).

A total of 94 Canadians won Britain's Victoria Cross. Then in 1993, the Canadian government created a *Canadian* Victoria Cross.

In Ottawa you'll find a monument to Canada's peacekeepers in front of the National Gallery.

WHAT'S AHEAD?

Canada has proven itself as a peacekeeper many times and in many places. The United Nations and other countries continue to ask for Canada's assistance when conflicts flare up and peacekeepers are needed to help settle difficult situations.

But the Canadian Forces are also making a name for themselves in disaster relief. When earthquakes, hurricanes or tsunamis strike, Canadians are quick to contribute and get involved.

International Helpers

Since 1947, the Canadian Forces have participated in more than 70 missions in other countries. Many of these operations were for the UN, but others were for the North Atlantic Treaty Organization, the Organization for Security and Co-operation in Europe and the Organization of African Unity.

In areas of the world such as Eastern Europe, the Caribbean and the Middle East, Canadians remove landmines and dig wells, protect human rights and destroy illegal weapons. For example, the Canadian Forces have worked for more than 20 years to try to bring peace to Sudan in Africa. They also helped people devastated by Hurricane Katrina in 2005. (The RCMP has supported peace efforts around the world, too and so have such organizations as Elections Canada and Corrections Services Canada.)

Currently, more than 3000 Canadian soldiers, sailors and air force staff are on missions in other countries. Usually about 8000 Canadian Forces members are either preparing to head off on a mission, working overseas or returning home. They have built a great reputation around the world for both courage and peacekeeping.

When Sri Lanka was hit by a tsunami in 2004, Canadian soldiers were there to help.

DART

Canada's Disaster Assistance Response Team (DART) was set up in 1996 to provide emergency help in disaster areas. The team, made up of about 200 Canadian Forces soldiers, gives basic medical care, produces safe drinking water and builds camps for refugees.

DART has helped disaster victims in countries such as Honduras, Turkey and Sri Lanka. Workers flew to Pakistan after the earthquake of October 2005 to help people who had lost their homes and families.

The Next Hundred Years

It has been more than 100 years since a war was fought in Canada (see "North-West Rebellion," page 35). Since then, Canadians have fought in conflicts elsewhere the world. Many men and women have sacrificed their lives for what they believed were important causes.

Most people would like to live in peace, with no wars or battles causing death and destruction. Until that happens, Canadians will continue to be called on to bring peace and stability to conflicts around the world.

Canadian Cadets march proudly through Ottawa on Remembrance Day.

(see "North-West Rebellion," page 35)

Canadian Courage

Some victims of war are not involved in the fighting. Civilians in war zones lose their homes, belongings and sometimes their lives. They may be wounded or their rights may be at risk. The United Nations High Commission for Human Rights (UNHCR) stands up for these victims. In 2004, Canadian Louise Arbour was made commissioner, or chief, of the UNHCR. She is the first Canadian ever to hold this important position.

Arbour had to be brave to take the job — the man she replaced had been killed in a bombing. But she knew the importance of her work. From 1996 to 1999, Arbour had represented victims of war crimes at the International Criminal Tribunal for Rwanda and the former Yugoslavia.

TIMELINE

1000

1000 — Vikings arrive in Newfoundland. Fighting soon breaks out with local Aboriginal people, the Beothuk (p. 6)

1500

1541 — French explorers clash with the Iroquois people in what is now Quebec (p. 7)

1600

1609 — Samuel de Champlain and his men join the Hurons in fighting the Iroquois (p. 7)

1628 — The English capture Acadia and Quebec (p. 12)

1632 — England returns Acadia and Quebec to France (p. 12)

1645 — Marie de la Tour defends the family fort but is overpowered (p. 13)

1649 — Saint-Marie Among the Hurons is burned (p. 8)

1650

1650–1658 — A peace treaty between the French and Iroquois stops the fighting (p. 8)

1654 — England captures Port-Royal and again controls Acadia (p. 12)

1660 — Adam Dollard des Ormeaux and soldiers fight a huge force of Iroquois at Long Sault Rapids (p. 8)

1667–1680 — The French and Iroquois sign a peace treaty and fighting stops (p. 8)

1670 — France regains control of Acadia (p. 12)

1686 — The English and French begin fighting over Canada's fur trade (p. 10)

1687 — The French invade Seneca territory and burn all their villages (p. 11)

1689 — Iroquois warriors attack French settlers in Lachine (p. 11)

1690 — Settlers from New France and First Nations soldiers attack English settlements in New York and New England (p. 10)

The English attack Acadia and Quebec but are forced to retreat (p. 12)

1692 — Madeleine de Verchères, just 14 years old, defends her family's fort against an Iroquois attack (p. 11)

1696–97 — French troops capture English settlements around St. John's, Newfoundland (p. 13)

1697 — Pierre le Moyne d'Iberville, with just one ship, battles three French ships in Hudson Bay and wins (p. 10)

1700

1701 — The Iroquois sign a peace treaty with New France and most of its First Nations allies (p. 11)

1710 — The English capture the French settlement of Port-Royal, rename it Fort Anne and call the surrounding area Annapolis Royal (p. 13)

1713 — France is forced to give up its claim to Hudson's Bay and Annapolis Royal (p. 13)

1744 — The French attack Annapolis Royal but have to retreat (p. 13)

1745 — The Fortress of Louisbourg is captured by the British (p. 16)

1748 — Louisbourg is returned to the French by the British (p. 16)

1750

1754 — The Seven Years' War begins in North America (p. 18)

1755–1762 — The expulsion of the Acadians (p. 15)

1758 — The British capture Louisbourg again (p. 14)

1759 — The Battle of the Plains of Abraham (p. 18)

1763 — The Treaty of Paris ends the Seven Years' War. France gives up almost all its land in North America (p. 21)

1764 — The Acadians are allowed to return to Acadia (p. 15)

1775 — Americans capture Montreal (p. 21)

Americans attack Quebec but lose the battle (p. 21)

1776 — American soldiers leave Canada (p. 21)

1800

1812 — The War of 1812 begins (p. 22)

1814 — The Treaty of Ghent ends the War of 1812 (p. 25)

1837 — Rebellions in Lower and Upper Canada begin (p. 28)

1838 — Rebellions in Lower and Upper Canada end (p. 30)

1850

1854–56 — The Crimean War in Europe (p. 31)

1866 — Fenians (rebel Irish Americans) attack New Brunswick and Ontario (p. 31)

1869–70 — The Red River Rebellion (p. 32)

1870 — Fenians attack Quebec (p. 31)

1874 — Royal Military College is founded in Kingston, Ontario (p. 25)

1885 — The Northwest Rebellion (p. 34)

1899 — The South African (Boer) War begins (p. 36)

1900

1902 — The South African (Boer) War ends (p. 39)

1914 — World War I begins (p. 40)

1915 — John McCrae writes the poem "In Flanders Fields" (p. 46)

1917 — The Halifax explosion (p. 49)

1918 — World War I ends (p. 49)

1936–1939 — The Spanish Civil War (p. 51)

1939 — World War II begins (p. 50)

1945 — World War II ends (p. 60)

1949 — Canada becomes a member of the North Atlantic Treaty Organization (NATO) (p. 65)

1950

1950 — The Korean War begins (p. 62)

1953 — The Korean War ends (p. 63)

Changing Place Names

Some countries, as well as some Canadian provinces and territories, have changed their names during Canada's history. In this book, the current name is usually used. Here are some of the older names:

- Ontario was known as Upper Canada from 1791 to 1840 and then Canada West from 1841 to 1867.
- Quebec was called New France from 1608 to 1763, the Province of Quebec from 1763 to 1791, Lower Canada from 1791 to 1840 and then Canada East from 1841 to 1867.

- Alberta and Saskatchewan were part of the Northwest Territories until 1905.
- Newfoundland joined Canada in 1949. Before then, it was a British colony, although it had its own government. Newfoundland changed its name to Newfoundland and Labrador in 2001.
- Nunavut was part of the Northwest Territories before 1999.
- England became known as Great Britain after 1707, when it united with Scotland.
- Russia was known as the Russian Empire until 1922. From 1922 to 1991, it was called the Union of Soviet Socialist Republics (USSR) or the Soviet Union.

Index